SWEET
SUCCESS
IN NEW HOME SALES

SWEET SUCCESS
IN NEW HOME SALES

Bill Webb, MIRM
on Selling Strong in Changing Markets

Sweet Success in New Home Sales: Bill Webb, MIRM, on Selling Strong in Changing Markets

BuilderBooks, a Service of the National Association of Home Builders

Courtenay S. Brown	Director of Book Publishing
Torrie Singletary	Production Editor
Koncept, Inc.	Cover Design
Circle Graphics, Inc.	Composition
Transcontinental	Printing

Gerald M. Howard	NAHB Executive Vice President and CEO
Mark Pursell	NAHB Senior Staff Vice President, Marketing & Sales Group
Lakisha Campbell	NAHB Staff Vice President, Publications & Affinity Programs

This publication is designed to provide accurate and authoritative information in regard to the subject matter covered. It is sold with the understanding that the publisher is not engaged in rendering legal, accounting, or other professional service. If legal advice or other expert assistance is required, the services of a competent professional should be sought.

—From a Declaration of Principles
jointly adopted by a Committee of the
American Bar Association and a
Committee of Publishers and Associations.

10 09 08 07   2 3 4 5

ISBN-13: 978-0-86718-618-5
ISBN-10: 0-86718-618-6
Printed in Canada

Library of Congress Control Number: 2006275480

For further information, please contact:

National Association of Home Buildeers
1201 15th Street, NW
Washington, DC 20005-2800
800-223-2665
Visit us online at www.BuilderBooks.com.

CONTENTS

Foreword . . . . , , , , ... vii

Preface ix

Acknowledgments xi

About the Author xiii

CHAPTER ONE
    Seizing Your Opportunity 1

CHAPTER TWO
    Emerging from the Pack 9

CHAPTER THREE
    Creating Positive Differentiation 17

CHAPTER FOUR
    Understanding the Gift 23

CHAPTER FIVE
    Applying High Touch 29

CHAPTER SIX
    The Mark of Greatness 39

CHAPTER SEVEN
    Delivering Sales Greatness 45

CHAPTER EIGHT
    Building the Sale 51

CHAPTER NINE
    Becoming a Sales Superstar 71

CHAPTER TEN
Organizing Prospect Management 85

CHAPTER ELEVEN
Providing Reasonable Sales Facilities 95

CHAPTER TWELVE
Getting Everybody on the Same Page 107

CHAPTER THIRTEEN
Organizing Sales Training 113

CHAPTER FOURTEEN
Presenting Guest Lectures 117

Index 141

FOREWORD

Beware! Bill Webb will change your life. If you don't want a large mirror placed in your face with all the imperfections of your sales technique and your company displayed, run now. If you don't want to analyze everything you are doing and accept the Bill Webb challenge to improve it, do not buy this book,

LifeStyle Homes hired him to do a two-day sales seminar in 2002. We wanted to improve our sales techniques. Well, I think we did some of that. Before the two days were over, we hired Bill to help us do an "extreme makeover."

He walks softly and carries a big mirror. Bill has the ability to demonstrate company weaknesses and challenge you to improve them. Maybe more important, he has the ability to see what you're doing well and help you build on your strengths.

Bill challenged us to decide who our target market was and to focus all our energies, advertising, and message at that one segment of buyer. This focus helped LifeStyle Homes in many ways. Today, our advertising, our internal messages to our staff, our public relations goals, our model merchandising, everything we do is designed to deliver the same message.

One of Bill's many talents is navigating between extreme personalities. He was able to use the best parts of each strong personality and work around the inevitable disagreements. This was a critical element in our growth.

Bill connected us with other leaders in the building community. One introduction was to Kay Green, MIRM, interior merchandiser, Kay and Bill talked our cost-conscious builders into trying Kay for one model. We now have the best model presentation in our county, and Kay does all our models. We would never have made that step without Bill Webb.

The LifeStyle Homes you see today is a strong, focused, viable company ready to meet the demands of a changing marketplace. Our advertising has a consistent message that our market is responding to. Our sales staff is well trained and growing in ability. Our construction staff is trained in the LifeStyle Homes message.

Financially, the rewards have been wonderful—far beyond my wildest dreams. My partner and I have been able to step back from daily company operations and become our Board of Directors. LifeStyle Homes is being led by strong young people who, you guessed it, have Bill Webb by their side.

In 2002, it was a very difficult decision to hire Bill Webb. Our company was just beginning to grow, and we were not being rewarded financially. We took the Bill Webb challenge, and I can say that it was worth every cent and all the effort. Bill has become a friend. He has enjoyed our growth and success almost as much as we have. My partner and I say, Thank you!

John Luhn, Partner
LifeStyle Homes
Melbourne, Florida

PREFACE

As is usual in my professional life, I was asked a number of times during 2004 to deliver an uplifting motivational speech to a group of new home sales professionals. I want you to know, it's a real challenge to pump up a bunch of people who are used to living in a golden time—the hottest residential market this country has ever seen! Everybody has been doing well, and many of us are new enough to the profession to have never experienced anything other than skyrocketing incomes.

While traveling to one such engagement in Atlantic City, New Jersey, it occurred to me that the time had come to develop a new message. I determined to challenge my audience of salespersons with the proposition that they might only be worth *minimum wage*. Because almost everyone in the hall that day had become accustomed to earning substantial six-figure incomes, the idea that they might be grossly overpaid generated considerable excitement.

They listened politely enough, but it was clear they weren't comfortable with my proposition. As a group, they felt they were working hard, and they had record sales to show for it. Flush with success, they were feeling pretty good about themselves. My message shook them up and made them think for a moment, but they probably reverted to comfortable complacency soon after leaving the hall.

Hence, this book. Speeches are a lot like Chinese food. The beneficial effect is soon lost unless meaningful behavior change occurs. Books get bought by folks who suspect there might be something of value inside. Books wait patiently for the moment to come when their message is relevant. Timing really is *everything*, and for you, maybe the right time for this book is *now*. That would make me very happy!

If you are a new home sales manager, your professional destiny will be determined by the performance of your team. If you recognize the signs of complacency in your own team, my hope is that you will read this book, take its recommendations to heart, and act decisively to save your career.

Make no mistake, the day of reckoning is approaching. No one knows when the next significant housing market shift will occur, but it's a reasonable bet that it will be downward rather than upward. When customers stop throwing money at us, weak salespersons will fail and their managers with them. This isn't my dream for you.

Your future deserves to be bright, brilliant even. And getting there should produce loads of fun and happiness as well as boatloads of cash. All you need to do is resolve right now to lead yourself and your troops in the right direction and in the right way. All through your journey to greatness, I'll be right here cheering you on and helping where I can.

Now, let's get to it, okay?

ACKNOWLEDGMENTS

Dan Levitan, MIRM	For originating this spiffy title and allowing me to use it
Bonnie Alfriend, MIRM, and Jean Ewell, MIRM	For twisting my arm until I agreed to write this
Samantha Webb, CSA	For believing in me and taking the ride
Don Hutson, NSA	For inspiring me to speak

The Terms, PERFORMANCE SYSTEM, BUILDING SUC-CESS In New Home Sales, Building The Sale, RUESAP, Prospect Action Control Software Systems, Prospect Action Control, PAC, and PAC 2001, wherever they may appear in this publication, are the registered trademarks of William N. Webb & Company, Inc. All rights reserved. Values And Lifestyles, VALS, and VALS 2 are the registered trademarks of SRI International, Inc., of Menlo Park, California.

The William N. Webb signature is a registered trademark of William N. Webb & Company, Inc. All rights reserved.

Bill Webb, MIRM, is a past president of the Institute of Residential Marketing of the National Association of Home Builders and is a winner of its Excellence in Education Award for his lifetime contributions to the Institute. Bill is the author of two of the four core courses required for membership in the Institute, *Understanding Housing Markets and Consumers* and *The Challenge of New Home Sales Management*.

Bill is a graduate of Woodberry Forest School in Orange, Virginia, and the University of North Carolina at Chapel Hill. He also holds an MBA in Marketing from the Kenan-Flagler Graduate School of Business at UNC. Bill is a former Naval officer and is a certified Master Scuba Diver and Divemaster.

William N. Webb & Company, Inc., is a nationwide provider of management, marketing, and sales improvement systems for home builders, community developers, and Realtors. For complete information on the firm's products and services, visit WEBBonline.com.

CHAPTER ONE

Seizing Your
CHANCE

Markets where customers rush into sales centers waving cash at us are *not* normal. If you've enjoyed working in an overheated market, I'm happy for you. I hope you have given appropriate thanks and saved some of your good fortune. Times change. Rates rise. Markets soften. Sales slow.

In normal new home markets, sweet success in new home sales doesn't come easy. Only those who are willing to work hard to improve their effectiveness do well. Helping you get ahead in your profession is the goal of this book. It will be your guide if you're ready to take the journey. This is your chance. Grab it.

Who

This book is for *you*. You may be a home builder who senses that financial success in home building requires more than knowing how to build homes. You may be a new home sales manager looking for new ways to fire up your troops. You may be a Realtor trying to be more effective working with new home clients. You may be a new home salesperson who aspires to become a super star. No matter which, you will find tons of useful information in this book and, hopefully, some inspiration as well.

I am going to speak with you as though you are actively engaged in new home sales or sales management. If you are really a builder, maybe a building company principal, please accept a special welcome aboard! Once you prove you can build a house and account for funds accurately, the next step toward making *real* profits involves taking charge of the selling process. I hope you are ready to do that.

What

This is a book about increasing market shares, profit margins, and personal incomes—all worthwhile goals, I believe. It will tell you what you need to know to be successful in achieving all three for yourself and your company. It will lead you through a series of action steps to get from wherever you are now to where you will need to be to maximize your potential.

All the good stuff I've learned from 30 years in the business is in this book. Within its scope, nothing is held back. I'm sharing the best of the best with you for the price of a book. What a deal for you!

What I ask you to bring in exchange is a desire to grow profession-ally—a need to be as great as you can be—not only to make more money, but to enjoy the exhilaration of knowing you are at the top of your pro-fession, fulfilling your destiny, and receiving the respect and admiration of all who know you.

Why

Everything you dream of for your future is at stake. You can either grow in professional capability and earn for yourself the rewards of superior performance, or you can drift along until changing market conditions take you down. The choice is yours.

The risk of failure extends to the company as a whole. Everything a building or development company does outside of the sales function is concerned with creating value. Finding land, sweating the entitlements, doing the engineering, building the infrastructure, designing homes, get-ting them built, everything you do is about creating value, but that value comes with a paradox attached. All the value you create has no value. In fact, the value you create will destroy the company unless it is converted into revenue. Because in business, only revenue has value. Only revenue pays the bills and earns you a living.

**Only revenue
has value**

Where does the value get converted into revenue? In the sales opera-tion, of course. That's why I am devoted to builders and building company principals getting actively involved in sales. Maybe it isn't the real comfort zone of many builders, but that's okay. Those of us in sales may seem a little strange, but we're decent people, and we want the company to do well. We would welcome our company principals becoming more involved.

Our immediate problem is that many of us have been reaching for the stars while standing in quicksand. We have been enjoying easy prosperity in the strongest market for new home purchases this nation has ever experienced. Personal incomes have been high and interest rates low, and our home buyers have been on a tear. It seems like everyone has moved up, buying as much house as they could afford while the golden opportunity has been there. In many areas of the country, there has been a desperation to buy we've never seen before.

A "Perfect Storm" of good things

Everybody in the home building and home selling business has done well, better than ever before for many. That is in part because immigration has been high. Motivated people have been coming to the U.S. to build lives for themselves. They are willing to work hard for low wages. That has helped keep prices down while increasing productivity in the economy. This has allowed interest rates to stay low, because there has been little need to worry about inflation. The great result for us is that businesses have done well, and lots folks feel rich and confident. They have been willing to spend lots of money on new homes. The fact that more and more households are supported by two or more income streams only makes it better. For home builders, we have been caught in the "Perfect Storm" in reverse: a once-in-a-lifetime confluence of demographic and economic benefits that has created a wonderful market.

Easy prosperity can breed complacency

The problem, of course, is that prosperity can breed complacency. Builders have taken their eyes off of sales because selling houses has not been a problem. Builders focus their efforts on land and entitlements and labor and materials instead. Their big challenge has been building homes fast enough to keep up with demand. For salespersons, selling skills have declined because they haven't been needed very much. Many salespersons have been overburdened and overstressed with the details of delivering the homes they've sold: picking colors, arranging financing, keeping up with change orders, etc. They've forgotten about following up with prospects and working on closing skills. The company has been selling as many homes as it can deliver to folks who are eager to buy. Why try any harder to sell any more?

In this reality, salespersons drift toward becoming order takers—brushing off the folks who *might* buy so they can write up the ones who are determined to buy *today*. Focusing on the ready opportunity is fine and a good business decision in the short run. But, in a truly scary way, it has become the norm for many salespersons, and that is extremely dangerous for them and the whole company.

If builders get the idea that it's easy to sell new homes, that no special skills are required, and that demand is infinite, they'll eventually attack sales compensation packages. They'll look for good people who will work for less than what established salespersons are accustomed to making, and they'll find them.

Showing and writing are worth minimum wage

"Not likely," you say? Well, I once sold out a substantial new home development with a sales force paid minimum wage, with no bonus and no override. I was able to do that because the product was *so* good that it really did sell itself. No sales skills were needed, only showing and writing. I was able to recruit really cool "showers and writers" from the nearest mall—good looking, eager, and pleasant salespersons who were used to selling perfume, jewelry, and shoes. They jumped at the chance to get into new home sales, and they ate up the training we offered. After starting with us, they went on to become quite successful in other communities as regular front-line new home sales professionals, getting paid full boat. You may know some of them.

In two days of initial training, I was able to teach them how to demonstrate the model home and fill out the paperwork correctly for customers who had decided to buy. In fact, their performance in demonstrating and writing was far better than I typically see on mystery shopping videos I review these days.

You might ask yourself this question: "If all salespersons really do is show and write, what makes them think they're worth the big bucks they're earning?" The sad answer is, "They aren't."

So, salespersons are grossly overpaid? Well, maybe. Certainly, there is ample evidence that in areas of the country where demand for new homes has exceeded supply for years (southern California, for instance) salespersons are typically paid much less per sale than they are in other places. This is simple economics at work. Salespersons are reckoned to be less important to the sale in these areas, so they command a smaller portion of the proceeds.

Architects and merchandisers are making YOUR money

Salespersons in high demand areas have often helped themselves lose out by conforming to the paradigm that says, "Don't accompany prospects on a model tour." This means they don't even show; they just write. This robs the model home of its point-of-sale advocate who matches its features and benefits to prospects' needs and desires. As a result, the model must have sufficient charisma to sell itself (every builder's dream). Architects and merchandisers are called upon to make every model home look better than every other model home. In turn, architects and merchandisers make the money salespersons could make if the salespersons would just get more involved.

This is disturbing to me. On one hand, I would be first in line to advise builders to cut sales compensation if salespersons aren't important in making sales. On the other, I know in my heart that for most areas of the country, out-of-control demand for new homes is a temporary phenomenon. Over time, the personal intervention of effective salespersons will be crucial to most home building companies. So, if we allow sales talent to wither away when markets are strong, we will be sowing the seeds of disaster later on.

Oh, I know salespersons would disagree with the idea that they are only worth minimum wage. They would say, "We do much, much more than show and write!" But, do they really? For many of them the much, much more has to do with order fulfillment, not selling. It's what comes after the sale that fills their time and depletes their energy.

Free salespersons to sell—please

I guarantee you we can hire good people to do the after-work for less than builders pay salespersons to do that fulfillment work now. "What?" you say. "Builders don't pay salespersons anything to do fulfillment work. It's included in the commission that's paid at closing. The fulfillment work is free. That's what's so cool about it. We know it needs to be done, but we don't have to pay for it!"

Oh, but you do. Builders pay for order fulfillment in the form of opportunity costs for lost sales. All the time and energy salespersons spend doing fulfillment work is time and energy not available to them for selling. Every time a sold customer comes back to the sales center, they risk interrupting a new sale in progress. What about the dissatisfied customers who storm into sales centers to complain about something they think is wrong with their house? Do they come in on Wednesday mornings when it's quiet? No. They come on Sunday afternoons so they can cause the maximum disruption.

Done right, selling is an extremely sophisticated art form that requires special talent and energy. Good salespersons are a lot like race horses. They can answer the bell time after time and accelerate to top speed. Asking them to pull a plow is a mistake. They aren't very good at it, and you're destroying a valuable resource when you make them try.

The truth is that the sales force supports the rest of the company. Without sales, everything else stops. Why would any rational business owner risk total company failure to get the troublesome fulfillment job done for free?

Maybe the answer is because there exists the underlying prejudice that salespersons don't earn their keep anyway. "They are overpaid and underworked. They come in late and leave early. They wear nice clothes, sit in air-conditioned comfort and drive expensive cars. Don't they secretly watch soap operas on company time?" It's easy for everybody to envy and resent salespersons. Therefore, "It's only right that we should saddle them with busy work. They have lots of free time."

As with many prejudices, there is some truth supporting this one. As with all prejudices, it is extremely destructive. I live to root it out! Lazy, uncaring salespersons are not to be tolerated. Get rid of them if that's what you think you have.

Help salespersons earn high incomes

My position is that selling talent is crucial to home-building companies. I would much rather help salespersons *earn* their high incomes than see them cut back for any reason—valid or not. That is the whole purpose of this book: to mobilize all involved, from builder-principals to sales managers to salespersons, in the pursuit of excellence. Let's all make fancy incomes, have a great time on the job, and do good work! Life is happier that way.

Assembling a team of eager, capable people and training them how to sell is the primary purpose of sales managers. Many builders assume their sales managers have done their jobs well because sales are happening. With slower sales, sales managers are the first to feel the heat of dissatisfaction and disapproval, and their team members are right behind.

Smart sales managers and salespersons are focusing on getting back in shape for real selling. The ones who do will survive and prosper. Others will fail.

Where

If you're looking for help, this book will be your principal resource for positive change. Something made you pick it up and read this far. For that reason alone, I am assuming you feel some concern about your professional future. I am trusting that you will take some reasonable action to assure a bright one for yourself and the people who depend on you. I am willing to do my best in these pages to help you reach your personal and professional goals. If you read it, really read it, you'll find the right path. If you're willing to act on what you read, I know you will gain an outrageous competitive advantage over your colleagues who refuse to change.

When

How about now? You've already started, and that's the hardest part of any task. Now, all you need to do is keep going, and good things will start happening to you right away.

CHAPTER TWO

Emerging from the
PACK

In chapter one, I suggested that the rising tide of a robust housing market tends to lift all home building boats together: the truly worthy, the okay, and the not-so-hot. If you are feeling pretty strong about your professional performance, you might want to make sure you have good reason, something more than just being a beneficiary of the rising tide. My bet is that you're the real deal, because I figure the pretenders threw down this book as soon as they caught its drift.

Anyway, if I am preaching to the choir a bit here, that's okay. Unless you are already leaning my way at least a little bit, you're not likely to implement many of the ideas I am going to propose. I would much rather believe you are staying tuned because you feel there may be food for thought in what I have suggested so far. If so, fasten your seatbelt. We're going to start building your outrageously wonderful dream future right now!

Good to GREAT

In the 300 pages of his best-selling book, *Good to Great,*[1] Jim Collins writes about two principal ideas. You can get them both in 30 minutes, so buy the book and get them.

The better of the two, in my opinion, is the idea that the enemy of doing great is doing good. Doing *good* is good. Doing good is profitable. Doing good is normal and comfortable. If not exactly easy, doing good is within your capability

---

[1]Collins, Jim. *Good to Great: Why Some Companies Make the Leap. . . . And Others Don't.* New York: HarperCollins, 2001.

without stretching too much. What possible reason could there be for leaving good behind to go for *great*?

**Long term, only great
will cut the mustard**

Well, my case is that residential salespersons who do good in strong markets will not be able to do good enough when demand for new homes has waned. In normal markets, doing good as we know it will not be sufficient to produce the results our stakeholders expect from us. When home buyers have stopped throwing money at us, only doing *great* as sales professionals will cut the mustard.

I dream about individual new home salespersons becoming inspired to go for great on their own. If that's you, go for it! If you are a sales manager, my dream for you is that you will grasp this idea and *lead* your team to greatness. It is, after all, a leadership challenge.

"The Karate Kid"

What would doing *great* require? The answer is simple, but profound. It comes straight from the movie "The Karate Kid." It's found in the paradox of "wax on, wax off." You remember it, don't you? The kid spends hours rubbing wax on, then rubbing the wax off again. In the beginning, he thinks it is all about putting wax on and then rubbing wax off. After a while, when his arms begin to tire, he wonders why he is being asked to do this dumb work. Then, as further time passes, it begins to occur to the kid that something else more meaningful might be going on, as surely it is. He is endlessly practicing arm motions he will need later on in his combat training.

Even so, there is still deeper meaning inside. Ultimately, Mr. Miyogi wants the kid to understand the symmetrical relationship between mastery of technique and focus on the opponent, because together the two inevitably produce victory.

**The Eastern way
is powerful**

There is probably not one among you who would bet on a south Philly street fighter in a contest against someone adept at Eastern martial arts. We've all seen enough kung fu movies to accept the inherent superiority of the Eastern approach to combat, but what makes the Eastern way better? I promise you, it is that combination of mastery of technique and focus on the opponent.

Surely, we all accept that there is a body of knowledge that defines Eastern hand-to-hand combat. It is an extensive body of intricately detailed knowledge, in fact. The process we know as qualifying for your black belt involves learning a small portion of that knowledge to a reasonable level of proficiency. Maybe it is mastery, maybe not. I can't say for sure, but you get the point, don't you?

Technique ahead of consciousness

Until you are thoroughly familiar with the specific techniques you may be called upon to use, your mind is still involved in remembering how to do each one. When it occurs to you to employ a given motion, you have to stop for an instant to recall again exactly how it is supposed to be done. In combat, that instant of hesitation can be fatal. To prevail, your knowledge of technique must be ahead of conscious thought—it must be instinctual. You must have mastered every technique you may need to use if you hope to win.

As you approach mastery of technique, a marvelous thing happens inside your head. For sure, your confidence in yourself increases, but that's not the big thing. The magic is that your mind is freed from thinking about what you ought to be doing, so you can concentrate on what your opponent is doing. You can center yourself, open the channels, and act instinctively on what you sense. As in jujitsu, where the main idea is to use your opponent's physical momentum to your advantage, the larger picture in all of the martial arts is to get ahead of your opponent mentally so you see decisions being made before actions commence. That way, by the time your opponent's blow reaches you, your countermove is already in place.

It's probably a Zen thing in that your ability to do this is never perfected, but the concept is clear. You leave your body spiritually, flow across the space between you and your opponent, and place yourself inside your opponent's head. That way, you know your opponent's thoughts before your opponent knows them.

What an advantage! Every bit of it comes from having mastered your technique so you can focus on your opponent.

Master sales technique— focus on prospects

In new home sales, we have no opponents, but we do encounter a continuing stream of new prospects. Each prospect presents a unique combination of direction, velocity, and spin. In the social interaction that ensues, both parties have an agenda. We want to sell to anybody. They want to buy from somebody, maybe. In this environment, the meaning of wax on, wax off becomes mastery of the technique—focus on the prospect.

Surrender to spontaneity

There is a body of knowledge that defines the profession of new home sales. It is extensive and intricate. I have devoted a huge portion of my professional life to gathering that knowledge and coming to understand how to use it. I promise that as you move closer and closer to your own understanding of that body of professional knowledge, you'll find the same two magic things happening to you. You'll see more and hear more from your customers, because you will be focusing on them rather than worrying about what you are supposed to do next. You'll also find that your rising level of self-confidence in your sales technique will allow you to surrender to spontaneity. Whatever happens next will be okay, because you'll know what to do instinctively, and you'll do it right without thinking.

We've all heard in sales training that there is special significance in our having two ears and only one mouth. The message just gets stronger when you consider that we also have two eyes. Listen and observe. Get inside your prospect's head. Then, act with confidence.

Customers routinely show and tell us how to convince them, but we generally miss the clues because we are focused on ourselves instead of them. Self-absorption is a peculiarly Western trait. The Eastern alternative is to focus on the other person—in the case of new home sales, the person with whom we're trying to create a relationship.

Most of us find that the sincere and respectful attention of another person is a pleasant thing. We automatically start thinking how neat the other person is, if for no other reason than they seem to think we're neat. You see rapport building going on here, don't you?

I submit the only way to truly focus on the customer is to have mastered your sales technique to the point where you no longer have to think about what you should do. You just keep doing the right things without conscious thought, because you have practiced, drilled, and rehearsed until you are blue in the face.[3] Until you have practiced, drilled, and rehearsed until you are blue in the face, most if not all of your mind's awesome power will be focused on you and what you're supposed to be doing, rather than focusing on the customer. You'll miss their messages, and you'll likely miss their sale.

Us or Them?

Another peculiarly Western trait in professional selling is to go after customers for our personal gain instead of helping them discover their own best interests. The norm in sales training is to focus on "the close." Closing is considered to be the most challenging part of selling, so good salespersons must become good closers, right?

We hear, "Start closing when they drive up. Continue closing as they walk toward your office. Keep on closing the whole time you are with them. There is no such thing as a trial close. Don't quit closing 'til they buy or die!"

Yes, that's somewhat tongue-in-cheek, but we really do hear things like, "What we need around here are real closers—master closers—six shooters!"

Isn't that saying it's all about us, all for our benefit? "Winning isn't the important thing. Winning is the only thing."

Folks who follow this path are likely to talk about things like "kill ratios." They sometimes refer to buyers as "liars" and prospects as "suspects." Their sales meetings often turn into brow-beating sessions, because overwhelming customers is recognized to be hard work. "You have to keep the troops fired up and scared of failing, or they'll chicken out for sure. The best ways to do that are to reward them in public and embarrass them in public. Always keep the pressure on. Make sure they're more afraid of you than they are of those prospects."

---

[3]Special thanks to Bob Schultz, MIRM, friend and colleague, for popularizing this important idea.

When we push,
they resist

Well, I'm all for getting more sales made, so I offer this thought. My experience is that when we push, prospects either close up or push back. Either way, we're likely to lose them.

To counter our skepticism, trainers prepare tricky entrapment closes they promise will overwhelm prospects. The tricky closes sound cool. Tricky closes sell books and tapes for sure, I guess because tricky closes promise easy solutions. Instant gratification is the American way, after all. "Just memorize these words, and say them convincingly. Your prospects will melt before you and sign anything."

Right.

Maybe tricky closes are popular because some builders and managers reckon that salespersons are pretty worthless anyway, so it's okay to pressure them into doing things against their nature. Maybe they feel it would be cool to have smooth-talking salespersons out front manipulating customers into buying homes they don't really want. I don't know about you, but I think keeping happy buyers happy is challenging enough. I don't even want to consider having to manage a herd of unhappy buyers!

The serious reason for the pervasiveness of tricky closes probably has more to do with cultural bias than it does any real desire to harm anyone. As Americans, we tend to believe in taking proactive action to capture what we want. Life, to many of us, is a contest that inevitably produces winners and losers. We intend to be winners. It's in our nature.

Do less,
accomplish more

So, it's not surprising that we place special emphasis on closing strong. It is the Western way, after all. The Eastern alternative would be to accomplish more by doing less. The idea here is that when we reach out to customers in sincere friendship, they will meet us halfway. As they learn they can trust us not to manipulate them for our own gain, they will come forth with all sorts of information that will help us determine exactly what their dream of living in a new home is. Then, all we have to do is portray their dream, place it in the home we wish to sell, and allow them to buy the package.

This friendship idea is not soft-headed altruism. It is the more direct path to sales success. To begin with, it emphasizes the positive aspects of buying and selling, not the negative. It takes the pressure off both prospects and salespersons. It frees both to be more like themselves instead of acting in some artificial way they think is expected of them. By being more respectful of both prospects and salespersons, the friendship approach removes the barriers that traditional selling pressure imposes. It is the easier, more productive way to sale success.

Its only enemy is cynicism.

By the way, when we meet, ask me to show you in real life a startling little demonstration of alternative closes that will prove just how well the friendship approach works. You'll laugh in amazement. Here's how it goes.

Push Me—Pull You Closing

Have your group stand up and pair off in twos, facing each other. Ask everyone to lift their arms to chest height in front of them with palms held vertically and facing outward. Then ask everyone to touch palms with their partners gently. Now, ask all participants facing left to gently press on their person's palms. Don't knock them down, just press ahead steadily.

**Respectful closing
is more productive**

Ask them what happened. The answer will be, "When I pushed forward, my person pushed back." What does that tell you about manipulative closing?

Now, ask all participants to stand in place as before, but drop their hands to their sides. Then, ask all participants facing left to reach out and shake their partners' hands.

Ask them what happened. The answer will be, "When I reached out in friendship, my partner met me halfway. What does that tell you about closing in friendship?

This little demonstration works every time, and I think it's really neat. It makes the point very clearly that pressure in closing produces resistance. On the other hand, genuine concern for the other person is always welcomed.

Maximizing Selling Power

Do you see how the idea of "mastery of technique—focus on the prospect" meshes with the other idea of "meeting prospects in friendship"?

It's easy. When prospects lower their defenses because they perceive no threat, they'll be even more open about telling you how to sell them a home today. When salespersons stop focusing on themselves, they'll get the messages their prospects send, and because they have mastered their selling techniques, salespersons will know exactly what to do to make the sale happen. Closing will still be important, but no abusive closes will be necessary. I promise you this works like magic!

CHAPTER THREE

Creating Positive
DIFFERENTIATION

I n chapter two, I introduced the idea of paying respectful attention to our customers' best interests so they would be inclined to meet us halfway in the sales process. This is much more comfortable, and more productive, than having them resist our selfish efforts to close 'em against their will. In this chapter, I will examine the principles of creating positive differentiation as a foundation for becoming truly GREAT professionals in new home sales.

The Commodity Approach

I am fond of shocking builders with the idea that new homes are a commodity. You recall, a true commodity is a product with no real or perceived differentiation. Wheat would be a good example. Once stored in their silos, Joe's wheat is the same as Julio's wheat, which is the same as Jane's wheat. The only factor that would influence you to buy one person's wheat instead of another's is price. In considering price, most people would instinctively search for the lowest price possible, perhaps even pitting one wheat seller against another by threatening to go down the road to buy elsewhere unless a significant price concession were to be offered.

Builders typically resist the commodity idea, because builders tend to think that their homes are better than anyone else's—if for no other reason than their homes are *their* homes. They sweat the details on their homes. They pour their effort into building their homes. Sometimes, they even risk the one they live in to build new ones for folks they don't even know. Builders tend to wonder how anyone could fail to recognize the obvious superiority of their products when so much of their genius has been poured into them.

New homes cannot avoid being similar

I have great sympathy for this position. And yet, experience shows that, from the customer's point of view, new homes begin to look pretty much alike after folks have been shopping for awhile. That's because competitive forces, market dynamics, and customer expectations drive new homes to be similar. No builder gets to enjoy the advantage of having a genuinely new and good idea for long before multiple builders copy it. All builders struggle with pretty much the same land, entitlement, infrastructure, materials and labor costs, trying to pack in as much attractive value as they can while staying within a given price range. Customers expect houses to have a certain look, delivering the right version of local architectural preferences consistent with their price. No wonder new homes in a given market area tend to look so much like each other.

Customers get confused

We know from experience that our customers get confused. They come back to see us on return visits looking for a home they think they "saw" at our model center, and we know it doesn't exist. That's because they have created a dream home in their minds made up of pieces of the real homes they've seen. They married Frank's living room with Mary's kitchen with Esteban's bonus room and Samantha's extra large garage. When they discover they can't have what they want, they fall into the commodity trap and go for a price concession. This is not good for either the builder's market share or profit margin.

Growing Share and Margin Together

My goal as a marketing consultant is exactly the opposite. My dream (and my objective) for my clients is to build market share and build profit margin at the same time. To some, this seems counterintuitive. The conventional wisdom in retailing is that you can have it one way or the other but not both ways at the same time. If you want more market share, by which I mean selling more homes faster, you must surrender profit margin and offer deals to bring 'em in. On the other hand, if you want more profit margin, which generally means selling at higher prices, you must accept a slower pace of sales as a trade-off. This seesaw idea is pervasive, but truly, it is only a paradigm that is routinely ignored by world-class marketers.

Both the good folks at BMW and the other good folks at Rolex understand how to get share and margin at the same time. There is no question that both produce a technically superior product. However, we might question the criteria upon which the superiority of Rolex is based. Certainly, it is not accuracy in keeping time. It has to be related to intricacy of mechanism and precision of craftsmanship, doesn't it? Can't I get a better timepiece at Walgreens for something close to $19.95?

Some people aspire to own the best only

Still, both BMW automobiles and Rolex watches are judged to be superior products for their intended uses. What sets both apart in terms of their marketing prowess is that both companies have induced large numbers of specially targeted consumers to line up to pay substantial premiums to possess their products. This is a huge idea!

BMW and Rolex are able to get people to line up to pay a premium price because they deliver something extra, besides function, that their customers value highly. They deliver pride of ownership, validation for hard work, an aura of prestige and power, or maybe just the promise of success to come. None of these things has anything to do with product function. They exist only in the minds of the buyers of these products. They are not real, but they motivate people to buy, nonetheless.

Intangibles often justify premiums

These two companies are great examples of using brand charisma to create positive product differentiation, and they have been marvelously successful exploiting their advantage. They have established their products as symbols of individual success in pursuing the American dream. Their purchasers imagine that people around them will think more of them because they own one of these products. That may or may not be true, but what is undeniable is that these same purchasers will think more of *themselves* because they are able to pay the premium. Even if in the actual buying, some purchasers wheedle for a special deal, their apparent ability to pay the premium—which is part of their public display—is an important component of the extra value they perceive these products deliver to them.

Going for Product Differentiation

So, we see that creating positive product differentiation in the minds of target market customers is an important step toward inducing people to pay a premium to buy our products. We also see how making that happen is the key to increasing market share and profit margins at the same time. Building brand charisma is an important method to use in creating that positive differentiation. It's better when the charisma is real because there truly *is* something special about the product. Remember, though, that the old adage "perception *is* reality" applies here. Just ask the folks at Lexus how they feel about the reality of BMW's technical excellence. You'd likely get an interesting response.

The viability of branding is a hot topic in new home marketing. Some support branding passionately. They believe it is absolutely possible to motivate a person to consider a builder's offerings based on that company's brand name and reputation. National builders live in this position. When you see a big newspaper ad that shows all the locations where a particular builder's homes can be found in a metro area, you're looking at an ad placed by a branding believer.

Other folks feel that home buyers first decide where in town they'd like to live and what price range they can feasibly afford, then they shop all builders whose offerings appear to meet their criteria. This approach is based on buyers' assuming that all builders and all new homes are essentially equal in quality relative to price. It's just a matter of finding one that pleases you esthetically.

Many smaller volume, local home builders rely on this approach, and some of them do quite well. Clark Rector, MIRM, a good friend and colleague of mine, used to tell the story of a small-volume local builder-developer who created a new community next door to one of the mega builders, who always ran large color newspaper ads. The local guy's entire marketing program was to place a sign out front of his neighborhood painted in the big builder's colors and typeface. The sign simply said, "ENTRANCE."

You might argue that this was an extremely sophisticated approach, but the reality for most small-volume builders is that they stay away from branding because they feel they lack the means or the understanding to go for it. This is unfortunate, because neither needs to be true. There are rich opportunities for local builders to create powerful brands for themselves. In fact, branding themselves well is their best possible defense against the onslaught of national builders.

Branding works for home builders

Having tried both approaches, I support branding where it is possible. The fastest (albeit, expensive) way to establish a brand is with artful display advertising. Perhaps the best practitioner of this approach is David Miles in Denver.[1] He works with builders across the country, and his material is top-notch.

Branding can also be established with public relations activities, especially when there is truly something distinctive about a building company that has relevance to the purchasing decision. One of my more wonderful client companies has a genuine connection of long standing to local public education. They establish their caring approach to home building in the minds of customers because of their caring approach to supporting local public schools (they donate large amounts of cash and supplies). We know our customers place great value on being able to rely on the company to do the right thing for them in building and backing their new home. Best of all, we know they are willing to pay a premium to receive that assurance. Every time a competing builder suffers in the press for some failing or another, our market share grows. It's very cool.

You can do even better with great salespersons

Although certainly effective, advertising and public relations are at best oblique approaches to creating the sort of positive branding differentiation that will achieve our twin goals of building market share and profit margins at the same time. That's because both of them are fundamentally focused on differentiating a product we've already conceded has many of the homogeneous qualities of a commodity.

---

[1]Milesbrand, 1936 Market Street, Denver, CO 80202; 303-293-9191.

A much more direct approach, in fact the cheapest and most effective approach, to creating positive product differentiation is to focus on your salespersons and their relationships with your customers. This is grand news for sales managers and salespersons, because it offers the chance to escape forever the threat of salespersons being marginalized in the selling process and having their incomes slashed as a consequence.

Didn't I start somewhere near that subject in chapter one and promise a solution? Well stand by. It's coming in the next chapter.

Meanwhile, try the ideas in this chapter. They work.

CHAPTER FOUR

Understanding the
GIFT

In the previous chapter, I focused on creating positive product differentiation in the minds of your customers so they will become eager to pay a premium to own one of your homes. Remember, we're trying to fashion a strategy that will lead to the long-term financial success of professional new home salespersons and their managers and principals—at least those who accept the challenge of leaving *good* to become *great*. Those salespersons who only care to show and write are vulnerable to income reductions. Sales managers who allow this behavior are candidates for replacement. Builders who tolerate shoddy sales performance suffer the appropriate punishment of lower profits. Because none of these negative states is acceptable, let's establish the guiding principle that *all of us will need to play the game of new home sales at a new and higher level.* Here's the next step along the path to attaining that level of professional joy.

The Prize for Victory

Before proceeding, pause for a moment to consider just what it could mean to your company's market share and profit margin if customers really did turn away from your competitors and lined up to pay a premium for the homes you sell! Everybody would win. Salespersons would make a lot of money to begin with, so they'd be happy. The sales manager would justly earn the credit for making this wonderful thing happen. Your marketing manager would be beaming, and so would your builder—all the way to the bank. Your construction and administrative types would be happy because their employment would be secure. Your customers would be delighted because they got exactly what they wanted and more. Your professional life would be truly wonderful.

Good News for Sales

My thinking is that this would be so cool that it is worth exerting some real effort to make it happen. Marketing-wise, you would move toward that goal by refining your architectural designs, looking again at your model merchandising, and paying fresh attention to your advertising presentation, all with your target customer's psyche in mind. But, the really good news is that you can do something right now that would be more powerful than any of those other things to bring this about.

It's more than the house

It's easy! All you've got to do is understand that a new house is not what your customers really want to buy. If you accept that transportation is not what a BMW purchaser really wants, and if you agree that a Rolex buyer is looking for a lot more than just a timepiece, it shouldn't be hard to grasp that a new home buyer is looking for something more than a new home. Oh, I know, that's what they say they want and that's what they buy, but as we learned from BMW and Rolex, there's much more to it than that.

It's the *gift* inside

We understand from consumer research that what they really want to buy is a very special gift that is not the house. Their gift is their unique dream of what their lives will be like when they are living in their new home. They've got a big neurolinguistic programming visualization thing going on without even realizing it (see chapter nine). Trust me on this, and grow rich on Tuesday. As magnificent as your house may be, it is not their gift. Your house is the *box* their gift comes in.

This means, that if you are caring enough to find out what their unique gift is, and skillful enough to place it in your box, they'll buy the package from you and happily pay a premium for the privilege.

You just have to understand how good this news is!

Point One: If your home is only the box, not the gift, it
doesn't really matter as much if customers think it
looks like your competitor's. (This tackles the troublesome commodity challenge.)

Point Two: Being able to make the sale at a premium by
placing their gift in your box makes salespersons
worth the big bucks they want to earn. (This backs you
away from those threatening pay cuts.)

Do you remember the successful sales staff paid minimum wage in
chapter one? They could not do the gift thing. They had neither the professional knowledge nor the skill to apply it. All they could do was show
and write. Showing and writing was only worth minimum wage to us. If
you've read this far, my bet is you are ready to get more for yourself and
your sales team by doing more to prove your value. Maybe you are bored
with good and you want to go for great. Hooray!

Let's examine the gift idea and see why it is so powerful. Every person shopping for a new home starts with a conceptual dream of what
their life could be like once they move in. As they get closer to making a
buying decision, their dream gets more focused and more specific. After
all, the whole process of shopping for a new home has to do with meld-
ing a fuzzy but nice image of the future with the reality of an actionable
opportunity.

Granite countertops are nice

Sometimes, exciting new possibilities for enjoyment surface during
the shopping phase and get added to the dream. Discovering the existence of granite countertops and deciding they're nice might be an example. Other times, the need arises to compromise a part of the dream to
make the remainder come true. Dropping the requirement for a bonus
room to accommodate the realities of credit scores might be an example
this time.

Anyway, as they get closer and closer to actually buying a home,
their dream becomes more real and more powerful, ultimately trigger-
ing the emotional urge to make it come true sooner rather than later. The
formerly hazy dream has now been transformed into a specific gift that
prospects will buy as soon as they find a home that delivers it.

Placing the Gift Inside

Here's an easy example to illustrate the power of the gift. Rod Peterson is moving to town with Jodi, his wife, to take over the helm at the First Local Bank, N.A. They have three children who will be occupying the home with them. They are looking at our Cambridge model with Ralph Emerson, our salesperson. The Cambridge is a two-story brick home with Georgian-style architecture. It has a killer family room overlooking a pool area, a gourmet kitchen with imported stainless steel appliances, as well as formal living and dining rooms flanking an impressive entrance foyer. It looks and feels like a bank president's home.

**Formal entertaining
requires catering help**

Ralph sealed the deal when he demonstrated how the pool bath could double as the bathroom the caterer's maid and butler could use when the Petersons entertain. You see, Ralph correctly surmised the Petersons' gift was their dream of "power entertaining" banking contacts at gracious cocktail and dinner parties—the kind of parties where Jodi couldn't possibly be seen doing any work in her gourmet kitchen.

It's even better when your ability to portray the gift correctly can resolve a hidden objection. Here's another example.

Mr. and Mrs. Johnson, Ted and Sally, appear to be in their late thirties. They are both employed and doing well in their jobs, Ted as a financial analyst and Sally as an advertising executive. They have two children, Martha, 9, and Ted, Jr., 13. They have come to our gated move-up community and are looking longingly at our Amherst model. It's an impressive home, with all the latest features, and they can just afford it with Ted's bonus. Still, they are hanging back.

Standing in the model, Rhonda Peterson, our salesperson, opens her sales presentation notebook to a pleasant-looking photo, and the Johnsons stroll over to take a look. The photo is a shot from an elevated camera looking down into a warm and homey living room with cream-colored carpeting. To the far left is a nice brick fireplace with a small fire burning inside. On the hearth, a honey-and-white cocker spaniel placidly sleeps. The center of the photo is dominated by two youngsters who are lying on their stomachs, propped up on their elbows, evidently doing their homework from school. In the foreground, we see both parents sitting in upholstered chairs, leaning forward, looking over their children's shoulders as if to help with their homework. This is a pretty nice picture of family togetherness, isn't it?

The message that photo conveys is that when you own a home like the ones we build, you will be able to enjoy these wonderful family moments with your children and fulfill your natural desire to nurture and guide them.

Help us see this is for the kids

Rhonda chose this photo to show at this moment because she sensed the Johnsons were dealing with an inner concern about their careers possibly shortchanging their children. Rhonda correctly defined their gift as, "If we owned this home, we would really devote quality time to Martha and Ted, Jr., in the evenings."

Rhonda really didn't have to say anything. She just allowed the Johnsons to have a quiet moment living the story the photo told. The close happened without a word being spoken.

Going for *Great* in Sales

In my judgment, both Ralph and Rhonda showed greatness in these situations by understanding the power of the gift and by knowing how to deliver exactly what their prospects wanted to buy. This wasn't about Ralph and Rhonda gunning down their prospects; it was about paying them respectful attention, as I discussed in chapter one.

When you care enough to find out what each customer's special gift is, you are showing your willingness to put their interests first. You're devoting your time, your energy, and your expertise toward helping them discover exactly what they want in their dream home and why. Once you know that, you can guide them toward making the correct decision for their own future. If you've done the marketing part right, there'll be a home in your product line that's perfect for them.

Branding and Charismatic Selling

Branding is a marketing technique designed to preload prospects to favor your product. To have any power, branding must promise consumers something that is important enough to cause special behavior. The behavior you want is for them to aspire to own your product and be willing to pay extra for it.

Charismatic selling, such as I described above, accomplishes the same thing more efficiently. Instead of broadcasting a message you hope is motivational, charismatic selling customizes the message so you *know* it's right and delivers it at just the right moment.

The best part of it is that it doesn't cost a whole lot. All you need are good salespersons, good leadership, and good training.

Part of that training should be devoted to understanding the root cause of its power. We'll do that very job in the next chapter on "high touch."

CHAPTER FIVE

Applying High
TOUCH

S o far in our search for ways to bolster the effectiveness of new home salespersons, I have advanced the idea that mastery of sales technique would enable us to focus on the prospect and that focus would enable us to pick up the buying messages that prospects routinely try to send us. I have said that meeting our prospects in respectful friendship would further open up those communication channels, and I have introduced the concept of the gift as the reason people buy homes. Now it is time to blend in another one of my favorite sales concepts, one that has proven to be a foundation of my understanding of sales as a profession, the concept of high touch.

As much as I would like to claim credit for originating the idea of high touch, I cannot. All credit belongs to John Naisbitt, who published a seminal book in 1982 titled *Megatrends*.[1] John Naisbitt is a prominent social forecaster who learned his profession working for the Office of Strategic Services (forerunner to today's Central Intelligence Agency) in World War II. His job then was to identify leading subjects being discussed in German newspapers and calculate the total column inches devoted to each. In this way, he could tell what issues were important to the German people at any given time and track how that importance changed over time. As a predictor of the will of the German people to continue fighting for Hitler, this work was invaluable.

---

[1]Naisbitt, John. *Megatrends: Ten New Directions Transforming Our Lives.* New York, Warner Books, 1982.

After the War, he turned those same techniques into a continuing analysis of the American social fabric, culminating in the publication of *Megatrends*. This book set out to predict the ten biggest social issues of the 1980s that would affect all our lives. Of the ten, his concept of high touch, as contrasted with high tech, turned out to be the big winner.

High Touch Balances High Tech

Here's why we care. We know now that the personal computer, personal pagers, the cell phone, and voice mail were all introduced in the 1980s. These tools and other similar high-tech inventions changed everything about how we live. Professor Naisbitt correctly predicted those changes and forecast that we would welcome them because of the increased convenience and productivity they would bring. He also correctly surmised that we would have to struggle a bit to figure out how to fit these new devices into our lives: each required new and different behaviors that weren't familiar to many people back then.

**High touch means
we care about you**

The concept of high touch sprang out of the concern over integrating the new high-tech approach to living. In a nutshell, high touch refers to our urge to act in familiar, comfortable human ways with other humans who appear to care about us, as opposed to having to think like a machine in order to operate the machine, which doesn't care about us at all.

Let's consider an example before we go on to apply this powerful insight. If you are younger than about age 30, you may not remember a time when phones were always answered by people. Trust me, they were. Voicemail was a new thing in the 1980s, and it offered the convenience of leaving a personal message in your exact words for your intended party to recover verbatim at their convenience. That part was good.

It also required you to navigate your way through a hierarchy of arcane menus that only make sense to machines. That's bad. Worse still is the implicit affront to your personal dignity included in the ubiquitous lie. It's not "because your call is important to us" that we installed this voicemail system, it's "because your call is a bloody nuisance, and it's a damned bother to answer" that we fired our human receptionist.

**For our benefit
invites resentment**

The truth is that voice mail was installed for the company's convenience, not the customer's. The calling customer must expend extra energy
and thought to accommodate the system's limitations, when they might
be thinking they deserve more.

Have you detected yet that I have an attitude about voicemail? If
you understand my point of view, we can laugh about it together. If you
totally don't get it, please stop for a moment and try. The fact that you are
used to it doesn't make it right, only customary. You would gain a huge
advantage for your company if you could find a way to pay your callers
more respect.

**For their benefit
excites enthusiasm**

That's the whole point about high touch as contrasted with high
tech. People recognize it and don't like it when they are pushed around
for the company's sake. They only go along, because they have no choice.
On the other hand, people love it and warm to it when the company
seems willing to go out of its way on their behalf. They cheer up, become
your friends, and spend their money with you.

Does this sound at all familiar? When we push for our sake, they
resist. When we offer friendship for their sake, they meet us halfway.

This is exactly the concept of high touch. And, by the way, high
touch proved to be so true through the years that John Naisbitt wrote
another book specifically about it in 1999.[2]

You can take the power of high touch to the bank. It will become
your unfair competitive advantage if you let it. If you don't take it to the
bank, you'll be losing that advantage to someone who does.

Implementing High Touch

How would you implement a better high touch approach? Well, I might
suggest a few ideas, but the basic principle is almost absurdly easy to

---

[2]Naisbitt, John, Nana Naisbitt, and Douglas Philips. *High Tech, High Touch: Technology and Our Search for Meaning.* New York, Broadway Books, 1999.

implement if you care to try. Employing high touch means being *polite* to customers and acting like you appreciate them and are eager to help. High touch emphasizes the inviting attraction of genuine human warmth. High tech, on the other hand, shields the company from customers, using the cold power of seemingly arbitrary policies and procedures to increase company efficiency at the expense of customers' convenience. A high-tech approach indicates that you regard customers as a bother and that you're trying to insulate yourself from them as much as possible. From their perspective, you're just being *rude*.

If you want to go for high touch, review your entire approach to customers and look for ways to make doing business with you more pleasant for them. Here are some big items you might want to consider.

Better Voicemail

Why not start with improving your voicemail system? At your company's headquarters, think about setting up a separate number that you publish for customers only. That will get subs and suppliers off your customer line, for starters. Have a real person answer the customer line with a big smile and a cheery, "Thank you for calling us. How may I direct your call?"

That last phrase is important. It alerts the caller not to tell the answerer the whole story, only to be passed off to someone who will need to be told the whole story all over again.

If the person the caller wants is available, make the connection. If not, ask the caller if it would be okay to connect them to their party's voicemail. That's the respect-for-humans way to use voicemail: no lies, no menus, no "If you know your party's three-digit extension . . ."

Avoid Customer Interruptions

A big part of showing customers that you appreciate them is being ready to receive them when they arrive. That means getting off the phone before they enter your sales center, for one thing. When customers catch you on the phone, they may first be embarrassed for having interrupted you. Then, if you linger on the phone, they may become irritated that they aren't being accorded proper respect. If they overhear that your call is personal, they have the right, in my judgment, to become angry.

No matter how important the call might be to you, from the customer's perspective, their standing there in front of you deserves priority. They made a greater effort to get to you than the person on the phone did.

Avoiding this trap is easy. First, arrange your sales center so you can see approaching customers before they open your door. This generally means placing your desk where you can see your parking area. This way, you'll gain some time you can use to get off the phone gracefully.

Next, tell each person you speak with on the phone that if a customer arrives, you'll have to say goodbye quickly, but you'll call them back again as soon as you can. Nobody will object to that if you tell them in advance. This way, you'll have permission to get off the phone without causing any upset before the arriving customers reach your doorway.

A Graceful, Gracious Greeting

It should go without saying that welcoming customers to your place of business pleasantly and with enthusiasm is required. That's why you need to get off the phone—so you can pay proper attention to the folks as they arrive.

Choreograph your welcome sequence

The most outstanding arrival sequence I ever witnessed was at a master planned community in Tampa, Florida. They had a great clubhouse sales facility to work with that featured a very large and elegant entry foyer behind an all-glass doorway wall facing the parking lot. There was a library table placed in the foyer with one chair behind it. The "up" salesperson was seated at the desk working on some papers in a leather portfolio.

As I walked the thirty feet from car to doorway, I could see this woman gather her papers into the portfolio and smile at me through the glass. As my hand touched the door handle, she rose from her chair and stepped around the corner of her table. As I approached her, she smiled, looked directly at me, held out her hand, and said, "Welcome to Terrabrook."

Perhaps your sales facility isn't that grand. That's fine. What really mattered in the Terrabrook greeting was that it was thought out in advance and choreographed. The idea was to make me feel special right from the beginning. Obviously, it worked. Surely, you can figure out how to create a similar effect in the facility you have to use. It's about thoughtfulness much more than it's about facilities.

Convenient Sales Hours

For most builders, their home buyers need to be employed to qualify, and frequently two income streams are needed to make it work. Knowing this, why do we turn around and close our sales centers at five or six o'clock on weekdays? Whose convenience is being served with this? Then, we complain about having too much traffic to handle on weekends. (Correction: We don't complain. We understate the excess traffic, so the boss won't put on another salesperson.)

**How many retailers
close at 5 o'clock?**

Might a better approach be to offer extended hours during the week so folks could drop by after work, or even on their way out to, or back from, dinner with the kids? That's what most other retailers do to serve their clientele.

We tend to say that won't work for us because of important personal safety issues. Also, our salespersons have family obligations of their own, so it wouldn't be convenient to stay open late. Okay. But could the real reason be that we don't want to be bothered by shoppers until they're really serious? Is there something about dropping by in the evening that fails the seriousness test?

Stop and think about that for a minute.

Could it be that we have an attitude problem? My bet is that all safety and family issues are solvable if we put our minds to it. With respect, as a manager, how can you cling to a paradigm that wastes salespersons' time during the week and overruns them with more traffic than they can handle on the weekends? It's an absurd idea on the face of it.

Besides, it has been my experience that most model homes can be made to look more inviting in the evening than they do in broad daylight. Ask any competent model home photographer. They'll tell you that you only get total control over interior lighting when it's dark outside. That's why major shoots are almost always done at night.

Better Fulfillment Service

Here's one I really wish we could solve. It's no mystery that the sales process has a big dose of magic in it. People routinely trust us with what seems like all the money in the world to them. They obligate themselves to 30 years of making huge payments every month. They risk their family's safety, security, and happiness on our representation that we will take care of them and do everything right.

Your salesperson meets them, forms a bond of trust with them, identifies their special Gift, and packages it for them in one of your houses, and they agree to buy. It's truly magic.

Exactly at that moment, any normal human being would expect you to say, "Thank you so much for placing your trust in us. Thank you for your business. Thank you for the opportunity to make a profit from building your home." We instead say, "You need to realize that from now on, there are procedures you must follow, actions you must complete in a timely fashion, and certain things you cannot do. Failure on your part with regard to any of these obligations will place you in default of your legal contract with us and will result in legal consequences against you, up to and perhaps including, suit for specific performance."

Until they sign something, we run after them like little puppy dogs, panting and whining with our tongues hanging out, nipping at their heels. As soon as they sign, we rear up like grizzlies, cross our arms, put on our meanest scowl, and start threatening them. Why is that? How have we not made *60 Minutes* with this story?

Turning prospects into problems

I once resigned from an otherwise great client company relationship because they finally convinced me that their marketing program only functioned to convert prospects into problems. The same customers who were praised by name in sales meetings were soon being cursed by name in production meetings. If it hadn't been so sad, it would have been funny.

If this sort of thing is going on in your company, maybe you'd better make it your responsibility to do something about it. If nothing else, it's destroying your potential for referral sales.

The Ritz-Carlton Approach

It would please me greatly if you would take your spouse or significant other and check into a Ritz-Carlton near you for a weekend. Tell the bean counters it's a write-off. You are going there to study the best high touch approach to customer service there is. I promise you'll learn valuable lessons that you'll be able use to your advantage back on the job. Cite this book on your tax return.

To begin with, you'll notice that every employee who encounters you will make eye contact, smile, and say, "Good Morning," "Good Afternoon," or "Good Evening," "Sir," or "Madam," as appropriate. If you ask for directions to any place on the property, they won't tell you how to get there, they'll walk with you.

Sell the customer exactly what the customer wants

Nobody at a Ritz-Carlton will tell you that you can't have something you ask for if it is humanly possible for them to provide it. "Don't say no," is a rule at Ritz-Carlton. Instead, they say, "My pleasure," and then they make sure to add it to your bill.

Personal service earns a premium

Their service credo is, "We are ladies and gentlemen serving ladies and gentlemen." Sounds quaint, doesn't it? Quaint isn't the point, however. Charging $400 a night for your room is the point.

Every Ritz-Carlton employee has a personal customer appreciation fund they can draw upon when they feel it is warranted. If your luggage is delayed on the way to your room, for instance, you'll find your bell person presenting you a complimentary amenity to make up for the inconvenience.

There are many more examples for you to discover on your own visit. It is clear, though, that the whole marketing strategy of the Ritz-Carlton organization is to make their guests feel truly special. They surround you with appreciation and respect. They hope you'll stand just a little taller when you walk in because you're feeling so grand. They have learned that their guests will not only pay top dollar to enjoy that feeling but return again and again to get booster doses. They read Naisbitt's book, and they took it to heart.

The Pervasiveness of High Tech

At the other end of the scale, I've had fun over the years telling a story about McDonalds to illustrate an early example of using a high-tech approach to becoming more efficient. Of course, everyone knows about the benefits of standardized menus and standardized facilities. My point has to do with their high-tech training to up-sell customers.

If I go into a McDonalds store (they don't consider them restaurants, you know) and order a Big Mac and a Diet Coke, the counter person will likely respond with a cheery, "Would you like fries with that, sir?"

Hey, I'm into sales training. There's good stuff there.

Just for fun, sometimes, I go up to the counter and order a Big Mac and a Diet Coke and say, "And that's all I want." Invariably, the counter person will respond with a cheery, "Would you like fries with that, sir?"

This proves they're not listening to me at all. They are just checking off items on the computer keyboard that correspond to product names they hear coming across the counter and asking about the next unlit key. I can accept that in a trivial purchase, but I'll be darned if that approach would be sufficient for me to select your company to build my home.

Making Your Choice

So, which approach would you prefer to follow in your new home selling business? Which seems to offer greater promise for your future? Which seems to have greater potential for increasing your market share and profit margin simultaneously? Finally, which approach are you following right now?

Plugging in the Power

You can tell, for sure, that I feel strongly about the rightness and the power of high touch in seller-buyer relationships. I suspect that part of my frustration is generational. I realize that younger folks have grown up with computers and have learned from the beginning how to think like machines. They don't even realize how they have been morphed to accept the machine's way of doing things. For them, this is normal, expected, and perfectly acceptable.

Older people know the difference in a real and personal way. In the extreme, they avoid computers, cell phones, and TiVo, perhaps because they are so uncomfortable with the special requirements modern technology places on them. Maybe they don't feel they need those extra conveniences. Maybe they're just embarrassed.

By far the majority of people seem to have embraced high tech, some without thinking, the rest with some effort. However, here's the real deal: Everyone responds positively to the application of high touch. Why would we not want to avail ourselves of that power when it is so strong and so inexpensive?

It's just about being nice to people and treating them as though you care. There is no subservience involved, only gentility.

More High Touch

You'll be glad to know that I have saved the best part of high touch for the next chapter. It'll be even more good news for you, so let's get on with it.

CHAPTER SIX

The Mark of
GREATNESS

Back in chapter three, we were concerned that market forces drive new homes to be similar to one another, at least from the customer's perspective. I suggested that the way to avoid the kind of price negotiations that characterize commodity sales would be to apply positive differentiation to our products. A powerful and inexpensive way to do that would be to focus on the value of the *gift* in the purchaser's buying decision. It is good news for salespersons that gift placement is so powerful, because it is a technique they can use to justify their value in making the sale.

More Good News for Salespersons

There's even more good news for salespersons. Customers may confuse houses, but *customers remember salespersons—* clearly and distinctly. They remember the good ones, the bad ones, and the truly wretched ones. It's true!

That's because each and every salesperson is a unique individual with extremely distinctive features, mannerisms, and personality. Maybe the most similar thing about professional salespersons is their manner of dress—hopefully, most of them present an appropriate version of business-casual attire.

There's another reason salespersons are more memorable than the homes they represent. All human beings are more experienced in observing other human beings than we are in categorizing the design features of new homes. We know what we're looking for when deciding whether we like a person, so we're pretty good at it. Because a salesperson could be a pain, we're especially alert from the very beginning to see whether evasive action might be required.

Instant Bonding

Probably almost every one of us has had the experience of meeting a salesperson in some store and quickly becoming at least temporary friends. The salesperson versus customer thing never quite goes away, but it quickly recedes into the background. You're just becoming comfortable with one another and starting to have fun together. Pretty soon, you're looking for reasons to buy something from this salesperson because it would be such a shame to end the fun time you're having on a downer.

This is a way of saying that customers will go out of their way to buy from a great salesperson, because it is such a wonderful experience just being with them.

Attracting "Be-Backs"

If your homes tend to blend in with your competitors' homes in the memory of your customers, but your salespersons stand out distinctly as individuals, doesn't it seem reasonable to think that great salespersons might generate more return visits for your company than your homes do? Great salespersons would tell us that this is surely true, and they would be right.

Often, what makes great salespersons great is simply that they are nice people to be around. Customers positively enjoy being in their presence. Such salespersons are superb at building rapport without even trying. They genuinely enjoy working with customers and go out of their way to please them. They're polite, respectful, enthusiastic, and cheerful. They are great advocates for their product and can't wait to share their conviction that their homes are the customer's best choice. In other words, these salespersons deliver high touch.

**The Master Chief
Pemberton effect**

Here's a personal example of how this works. I once met a tall, fit, proud, and regal African-American salesperson at a local automobile dealership. I tell you, this guy was impressive in a very positive way. In response to my opening question about a new model not yet available for sale, he ushered me to the sales manager's office to look for a flyer. The manager was out, so we both went in to look around. While in the office, he said these magic words.

"I have to apologize for the appearance of this space, sir. We really need to get in here and repaint these bulkheads."

He sent me a secret message embedded in those two sentences, and I got it because I had the cipher. Did you get it? You would have, if you had been in the Navy like me. You see, in the Navy, rooms are spaces and walls are bulkheads.

Why was this message so great? Because I was wearing jeans on this Saturday morning, and I had on my old khaki Navy belt with the officer's crest buckle. He saw that, and rather than blurt out something trivial, he chose a more subtle but powerful method to make his special connection. Within a few minutes after that exchange, we had established that he was a recently retired master chief petty officer boatswain's mate. You have no idea what respect former Navy lieutenants have for master chiefs.

Pretty soon, we were discussing when we might have been in the same place at the same time but on different ships. We reminisced about which admirals knew their stuff and which were stuffed shirts. We talked about which ships were steamers and which were yard queens. Of course, we agreed all "brown shoes"[1] are weird. We even traded stories about playing with the Soviet Navy and how much fun it is to do that when nobody's shooting.

Within a few minutes more I found myself standing in his company looking at the most butt-ugly new car I may have ever seen in my life, and *I wanted to buy it!* Not because of the car but because of my need to affirm my respect for this gentleman's whole life by buying something from him. I didn't buy it. I surely did want to, though.

A great salesperson is more powerful than the product

The gift of this remarkable experience to me was the realization for all time that the *salesperson can be more powerful than the product in mak-*

---

[1]Naval aviators are granted the distinction of wearing brown shoes with their summer khaki uniforms. Real Naval officers, those who drive ships, wear black shoes. It's a subject of much good-natured banter between the two groups.

ing a sale. I'll bet you've had this happen in your life. Either you have bought something in a store just to reward the salesperson who has been so nice, or you have had someone buy a new home from you because you really bonded as friends. It's a common phenomenon that marks the presence of a great salesperson. We can use this to our advantage.

The Epitome of High Touch

Since that day, this principle of high-touch selling has been known in my world as the Master Chief Pemberton effect, and so may it be known in yours. You see, he did everything right. When I asked about an unavailable model, he didn't slough me off. He said he'd seen the same ad on TV and was curious about it himself. "Hey, let's go see if we find out any more about it together," was his approach. Then, he picked his time to send me his special message. Talk about rapport building: this was the Super Bowl of rapport-building. Then, he guided me over to that particular car. For all I know, the salespersons on duty that morning had a special bet going on to see if anyone could sell it. It was the most sport-oriented car on the lot that day, and I had asked about a sports model, but wow, was it ugly!

The Experience Rules

Years later, I read an interesting consumer research paper on the subject of the shopping experience versus product attributes in governing purchase decisions. The result of the research project was crystal clear. In any situation where the purchaser has to interact with a person selling the product or expose themselves in some way to the selling organization (entering their store or calling on the phone, for instance) the experience the customer has leading up to the point of decision is tremendously more important to the decision than the perceived value of the product itself. This is consultant-speak for, "People will walk away from the purchase of an item they really need if the salesperson makes them mad."

So, our job in the new home sales business is to create wonderful experiences for our customers when they visit our sales centers. If we do this, they will be much more likely to buy from us today or return to see us again after they have endured the indifference of other salespersons who don't care.

Obviously, Master Chief Pemberton was a wizard at creating my perfect experience. But even he couldn't overcome that aspic-red, brick-shaped Volvo with black spoke rims and a yellow maple dash. Come to think of it, they *must* have had a bet going.

Jai-Alai Versus Baseball

My experience with the master chief was also an excellent example of another important new home sales principle, the one about playing jai-alai with prospects, not baseball. We've already mentioned that prospects come into your presence with their own combination of direction, velocity, and spin. The same is true of the ball in both jai-alai and baseball. In baseball, the idea is to hit the ball square on the nose and send it over the fence. In jai-alai, however, you catch the ball in that long curved wicker basket (the cesta)—absorbing the ball's velocity more or less gently—and then you fling it back at the wall as hard as you can with the direction and spin you think will do you the most good.

I submit that you're showing more respect to the jai-alai ball than you are to the baseball, and that's the point. Gracefully absorbing prospects' initial approach before gently adjusting their speed and spin in a more useful direction is another mark of greatness in selling, and incidentally, it's the number one reason why a sales center should always be the first part of a model home presentation that prospects encounter. Salespersons need time and space in which to make that adjustment before prospects get to see what they came for—the pretty model home décor. So, in a sense, your sales information center is your cesta.

Master Chief Pemberton took at least 15 minutes to absorb my approach in a friendly, upbeat way, even though he knew he couldn't sell me the car I asked about. He was banking on his ability to switch me off onto something else, once he took control. He almost succeeded.

It's All About Attitude

How many times have you heard that one? Yet, it is so true. All of the high-touch power in the world will do salespersons no good if they don't have the proper attitude. Master Chief Pemberton certainly had it.

This book is overwhelmingly focused on developing selling skills. Skills are teachable. Attitude most likely isn't. You either have a good and positive attitude, or you don't. How would you and your fellow team members rate on the attitude scale?

**Positive attitudes
are priceless**

You have to love what you're doing, be proud of the company you represent, be happy at home, and feel great about the future. Most of all, you have to care about people, especially your customers. If you are their manager, I'm sure you can rate each of your salespersons on an attitude scale in a heartbeat. I want you to do that right now. Don't kid yourself. No wishful thinking is allowed. Now is the time for absolute truthfulness.

**Lose the
negatives**

I am asking you to take this journey toward future success based on a new approach to selling. If *your* attitude were the problem, you wouldn't have gotten this far. If you have salespersons whom you know will not accept this new approach because they have accumulated too many scars, you will need to help them find new opportunities. If you don't rid yourself of their negative influence, they will surely drag you down. This is especially true if the person you're worried about happens to be your top producer. I feel so strongly about this that I have included a special chapter on releasing unhappy salespersons later in this book.

Closing the Circle

For now, though, let's turn our attention to a more positive subject. In the next chapter, I'll share with you the way you can close the circle on all the subjects we've been discussing so far, using a high touch approach to insert the gift that your mastery of technique and focus on the customer has identified into a home they will buy today. You'll love it!

CHAPTER SEVEN

Delivering Sales
GREATNESS

So far in our search for increasing market share and profit margin for our builders, we have advanced the proposition that truly good salespersons can be more important to making a new home sale than the home itself. This is because salespersons affect prospects' minds more than the homes they represent. Salespersons are unique as human beings, bound together only by loose conventions of acceptable grooming and professional dress. Other than that, they are wildly different! They vary greatly in their abilities to connect with customers and influence their choices.

Salespersons are more memorable than homes

The homes they represent, however, are often so similar that customers sometimes get confused about what they saw and where they saw it. This is because all builders struggle with fundamentally the same costs, building restrictions, and consumer preferences to build in as much value as they can and still make a profit when the home sells. This drives competitive houses within a given price point to look and be a lot like each other.

Forgive me, please, for using a military comparison to illustrate my point. If you were to park a U.S. Air Force McDonald-Douglas F-15 Eagle fighter aircraft alongside a Russian Air Force Sukhoi SU-27 Flanker, you'd be amazed how similar they are. That's because the realities of aerodynamics at twice the speed of sound are the same for Russians as they are for Americans. To go that fast and carry along all that is necessary to go that fast and fight, the two aircraft end up looking a lot like each other—so much like each other, in fact, that if we were to remove the markings, most civilians wouldn't be able to tell which is which. Forget for a moment, the Russians probably stole our plans. That only shortened their development time. They'd have arrived at the same place all by themselves. They have excellent aerodynamicists there.

Your Wonderful Advantage

Trust me. All this is extremely good news for those of you who earn your living selling new homes, but only if you care to exploit the advantage that is lying there for you to pick up. Every time you use your unique abilities to convince a customer to choose your home rather than a competitor's home, you will be adding directly to your company's market share and profit total, and this is what will make you worth the big bucks you want to make.

You might ask, "Isn't this what you sales trainers have been saying all along?" Yes, but there's something new. Up to now, most of us trainers have been talking about doing something *to* the customer to make the sale. That would encompass all the hype surrounding the concept of closing. Master closers are trained to overwhelm customers into buying. It may be a frontal attack or a slick maneuver, but the underlying intent is the same.

What's new in this discussion is the idea of equipping salespersons to do something to the *house* to make it more attractive to customers standing there right now. I don't mean painting walls or offering to move them. I mean training salespersons to use the power of artfully chosen words and ideas to remake the house from what it is into what customers would want it to be that would make it uniquely perfect for them— placing their gift in your box so they will want to buy the package and pay a premium price for it.

Motivation Defines the Gift

In landmark consumer research, SRI International, of Menlo Park, California,[1] established that there are three types of consumers in terms of how their personal values affect their product purchase decisions.

---

[1]Values and Lifestyles (VALS) program: SRI International, 333 Ravenswood Avenue, Menlo Park, CA 94025; 650-859-5386.

Two of those three typically dominate our universe of new home shoppers. Principle-oriented consumers live to do the right thing and make responsible choices. The political label, family values, was created for principle-oriented consumers. They are duty conscious, and one of their main duties is to provide a safe, secure, and nurturing home life for their children. Because principle-oriented consumers work hard to identify and do the right thing, they tend to be a bit judgmental about folks who apparently follow a different path.

One of those other groups would be status-oriented consumers, who are motivated to gain the respect and admiration of people they respect and admire. Status-oriented consumers work hard to accomplish significant things so they can earn this respect. Along the way, they like to buy products that have brand charisma, so they can add the product's charisma to their own charisma collection. Hence, the special attraction some folks feel toward BMW automobiles and Rolex watches. Status-oriented consumers tend to be more forgiving about what other people do, so long as they themselves get what they think they deserve.

Lest there be any uncertainty, we are considering psychographic profiles here. The short message is that psychographic preferences drive product purchase decisions and thus produce powerful opportunities to target specific market segments with products that have magnetic attraction. It's *very* good stuff.

Guiding Architectural Appeal

One of the big uses of this consumer research insight is in targeting your home designs to folks you want to sell to. Principle-oriented consumers generally prefer a home that is pleasant in design but understated—friendly, if you will. The home should say, "Nice people live here who you would like. Why not drop in to meet them? They'd be glad to see you." Front porches are a great way to deliver that message. Wood is a good siding material to use; cedar shake siding in a Cape Cod style is smack-dab on. Inside, the home needs to be warm, inviting, and practical. Soaring ceilings are not appropriate.

Friendly versus imposing

For status-oriented buyers, the architectural preference is quite different. For these people, the home must be impressive and imposing. It needs to say, "Important people live here, and if you knew them, you would be important, too. Perhaps they will invite you in someday." Two-story homes are appropriate for this buyer because they deliver a sense of mass. Interior drama and elegance are encouraged. Too much is not necessarily enough in terms of ceiling height and architectural embellishment.

As marketing professionals, we respect all preferences

Even though you might think there is a moral high ground here, remember that as marketers, our job is to respect all dreams held by all people equally. We are not here to preach, but rather to sell. Our function is to like what our customers like.

These alternative themes are possible to deliver in a variety of price points and regionally acceptable architectural idioms. The opportunity for marketers is to pick your target profile and then go for it. If you have been successful selling primarily to one or the other profile, build on your strengths and sharpen your appeal for that one. If your success has included roughly equal shares of both, then you can decide whether to blend both messages into each house design or have different houses for different people. Sometimes by having a rich options and upgrades program, you can offer people the chance to create their preferred psychographic presentation within the base house, which is neutral. Because all marketing is test marketing, you can then test these ideas and see what happens.

Selling Psychographics

For us right now, the opportunity is to use the special skill and energy of great salespersons to take advantage of yet another component of our growing body of professional knowledge—the power and pervasiveness of consumer psychographics—as a selling tool. Here's an example of true magic in selling.

Today is Saturday, and it's chilly outside. You are standing in your sales center eagerly awaiting the chance to show off your charismatic model home that has two powerful free-standing columns marking the transition from entry foyer to living room. Those columns are very impressive! Your status-oriented buyers love them.

Up drives a late-model Saab. Out gets a fortyish gentleman dressed in a plaid woolen shirt and cords. He's wearing leather deck shoes, and he's smoking a pipe. A woman of similar age emerges, wearing a white blouse, navy sweater, maroon woolen skirt, knee socks (I still love those), and penny loafers. Right away, you're thinking, "Traditional, independent-thinking, not flashy."

Turns out, he's a professor at the university, and she is the administrator of the local blood bank. You're thinking, "Highly educated and professional; focused on giving back to society, not interested in making big incomes. Could be principle oriented. Probably aren't going to like those columns in my model; they'll see them as being pretentious. I know how to handle this."

You accompany them on the model demonstration tour (already left a bunch of you guys out, didn't I?), and you gracefully slide into a relaxed position standing directly in front of one of those columns. You're covering up as much of it as you can, but it's still coming out of the top of your head. The other one is flapping in the wind, so to speak. Having practiced, drilled, and rehearsed until you have mastered your craft,[2] you are focused on your customers. You wait for the flicker of disapproval that registers on the face of one of them when looking at that exposed column.

Change the model home on the fly

When you see it, you say, "You know, Dr. and Mrs. Johnson, a number of our home owners, who otherwise love their new homes here, thought we went just a bit over the top when we placed these columns in our model. So, we have worked out a no-cost swap to delete them in favor of placing a state-of-the-art recycling center in the kitchen. Would that perhaps be of interest to you?"

Stop and consider this for a moment, please. What has just happened is huge!

First, you cared enough about your customers to go with them. Because you did, you had the opportunity to customize your model home for them. Because you were professional enough to have studied and mastered consumer psychographics, you knew just *how* to customize it for them. Finally, because you had mastered your craft, you were free to focus your attention on them and look for the sign.

---

[2]Special thanks to Bob Schultz, MIRM, friend and colleague, for popularizing this important idea.

This is truly delivering sales greatness. In my sales coach role, this is what I live for. It brings me great joy when salespersons care enough to operate at this level.

More than that, this is worth big compensation. This sale would have been lost except for your intervention. All the money that was spent on architectural design and model merchandising produced a home that was unsalable to these buyers. You changed it on the spot into a home that delivered the *gift* they were looking for—a home that expressed their strongly felt environmental concerns, concerns that almost certainly would not have come up in typical qualifying, but which could have been predicted with high certainty from the other more obvious aspects of their principle orientation.

This is a higher order of selling than is normal in our business. This is almost certainly a higher order of selling than most new home markets require as this chapter is being written. It represents something important nonetheless: a mastery of technique, focus on the customer, and dedication to excellence that typifies the transition from good to great[3] that we decided back in chapter one might be worth shooting for.

Are You Willing?

The question now is whether this appeals to you as a method of operation. If you'd like to be this good, there is a path for you to follow. In the next chapter, I'll share it with you.

---

[3]Collins, Jim. *Good to Great: Why Some Companies Make the Leap. . . . And Others Don't.* New York: HarperCollins, 2001.

CHAPTER EIGHT

Building the
SALE

I promised to share with you a plan for making the transition from good to great as a new home salesperson. Helping your salespersons make that journey is the responsibility of sales managers, and it's a challenge I hope managers will soon accept. It's my belief that good won't necessarily be good enough when the housing market slows from its present record pace. When buyers regain their equilibrium because interest rates have risen, builders will turn more of their attention toward the sales process, and they may not be happy with what they find.

Builders believe we persuade customers

It has been my experience over 25 years, or so, that builders believe their salespersons *persuade* customers to buy. Because they feel that persuading someone to buy is demanding, they agree to pay rather generously for salespersons who appear to have that ability. If they only knew how little persuasion actually takes place, they would be less willing to pay so much.

My case is borne out in market areas where builders know that persuasion isn't a factor. In those areas, salespersons are paid substantially less than they are in other areas of the country where they actually influence buying decisions and thus affect their company's performance. That is to say, when builders no longer believe sales skill and talent make a difference, they become unwilling to pay for it.

That's as it should be. So, in good markets or bad, the best thing a new home sales staff can do to prove their value is persuade customers to buy. This means they actually connect with customers, gain their trust, and convince them that their product is the customer's best choice.

Customers are buying homes in spite of us

I have watched enough mystery shopping tapes to make myself truly sad on this point. It is common to witness well regarded salespersons failing to pick up obvious buying signals coming from the shoppers. It is almost unheard of to come across a tape of a salesperson who senses a selling opportunity and goes after it. That's one of the reasons I feel so strongly about mastery of technique—focus on the customer. I rarely see salespersons paying more than cursory attention to customers. It's almost as though salespersons regard customers as interruptions. It easy to see their discomfort as they try to figure out what to do next. No mastery, no focus, no confidence, no close. Yet, people are buying in record numbers. Go figure.

You know already I am against tricky closes. That's because I think most salespersons cannot bring themselves to use them. If they did, I'd feel bad for the customers. Because they don't, but maybe think they should, I feel bad for the salespersons, who are caught in a needless trap of guilt and frustration.

So, closing with verbal tricks is out, but failing to close at all is not right either. Turning away from our professional duty to be strong advocates for our builders' homes will get us all in trouble. The answer, in my judgment, is adopting a sales presentation plan that makes it easy to close well when closing is justified—easy for the salesperson and easy for the customer.

Closing becomes easy when you plan for it

One of the primary responsibilities of a sales manager is to specify the company's sales plan. Winging it on personality alone doesn't qualify. It is much better to have a basic plan for organizing the presentation so that information any reasonable prospect would need to make a buying decision is included for sure. The plan must also help salespersons learn what they need to know about the people they're presenting to, so the information they impart can be customized to the needs and interests of each individual prospect. This is basic to placing the gift the prospects will buy into the home you'd like to sell.

Here is such a plan. It's called Building the Sale™. It is a very good plan, developed here at William N. Webb & Company, Inc., and I heartily recommend it to you.

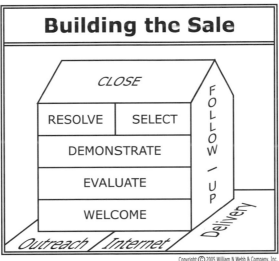

The premise of this sales presentation plan is simple, but profound. The best way to build a sale is from the bottom up, just as you would build a house. You cannot close until you have satisfied the other requirements of selling any more than you could hang the roof of a house in midair with no supporting structure underneath. When you've done the necessary prep work in Building the Sale, there is a clear sign that it's time to close. Just turn around and look for your customers. If they are standing there with you, it's time to close. If they aren't standing there with you, it isn't time to close. By leaving, they have clearly indicated that either what you have doesn't excite them or they don't like being with you. Oh, well, let's work toward a better outcome next time.

A review of the steps may be helpful. What you'll read here is an introduction to each. Don't get lost in the detail. For now, seeing how the process flows is the important thing. In a training session, I would cover step each in much more detail, which, of course, I'd like to have the opportunity to do for your group.

Welcome

The actual selling process, at least what we experience when we meet new prospects face-to-face, commences with sincerely welcoming your visitors to your premises, gaining the information you want from them, and beginning the process of establishing control over the sales presentation to follow. The welcoming process is also your one opportunity to make a good first impression, which is the vital high touch way to start building rapport.

Exercise control without appearing to have control

We've already touched on some of the warm, genuine, and respectful aspects of effective welcoming. You know from previous chapters that being ready to welcome arriving prospects is vital, but the control aspect is new. Because salespersons are there to accomplish a specific purpose, they need to be in control of what happens. Establishing that control without abusing customers is an important piece of sales technique that will have to be mastered. You're making a good start when you design your selling process so that customers want to do what you want them to, so you never have to force anything.

Evaluate

Once greetings and names have been exchanged, it is time to focus on evaluating your customers' buying potential. Learning each customer's RUESAP profile is the objective here. RUESAP is a memory aid that stands for **R**equirements, **U**rgency, **E**xperience, **S**ituation, **A**bility, and **P**ersonality. How can you possibly know how to help your customers until you know who they are, why they're here, and what they want to do?

Requirements refers to what your customers are looking for in the physical features of their next home. How many bedrooms and baths do they want and how much garage space? Do they need a bonus room, home office, or hobby room? Is a suite needed for an older generation? The general size of the home and its configuration in one or two stories is important. The specificity of answers you get to questions about requirements will likely have a great deal to do with your overall evaluation of buying potential. Customers who know almost exactly what they're looking for may be a lot closer to buying a home than those whose requirements are less clear. The answers they give you will go far in determining what their special gift is.

Urgency has to do with how soon customers could view themselves making a buying decision. It's a measure of where they are in the decision-making process. An occupancy target date can figure into this, but often it is even more useful to know how seriously they appear to be shopping and how far along they've gotten in doing their due diligence. Of course, if they're in town to buy a home this weekend because of a job transfer, there probably won't be much time for being casual or deliberate—either for them or you.

Experience involves their familiarity with the home-buying process and the scope of competitive shopping they've done this time around. Obviously, you would speak in different terms to first-time home buyers than you would folks purchasing their fifth house, because you'd want to be sure the first-time people understood their roles in the process. It's good when they know what a mortgage loan is.

Your customers' knowledge of your competitors is extremely important. In my world, I'd love it if they had already been to see my number one, two, and three competitors. It would be even better, if they had found a model they liked at one of them. That way, I'd know exactly what I had to beat to get their business. The circumstances are less favorable if they have just begun shopping and really haven't been anywhere significant yet. Closing buyers who haven't looked around much is especially challenging, although not unusual and certainly not impossible, but challenging nonetheless.

Situation refers to the circumstance that brings customers into the market looking for a new home. Are they moving up or moving down, closer in or further out? Are "nicer" and "newer" important motivations? Is the school district a motivator? Is commute time to a job an important consideration? Did they just get a bonus, or is another child on the way?

Generally, what they are trying to accomplish in buying their next home results from their situation. It's clear that early answers to situation questions will give you more insight into what their unique gift might be.

Ability to buy, of course, has to do with financial qualifications. There is no professionalism involved in spending lots of time with prospects who cannot afford to buy from you. Depending on your target market and price point, you may be able to broach this subject directly, asking them flat out if they have any money. More often, you will be relegated to observing quietly and making judgments on your own. Still, if there is doubt, you have got to satisfy yourself that proceeding is a good decision.

One of my good friends and colleagues, Tom Richey, MIRM, recently rocked my boat with this observation. A large-volume national builder ranked their salespersons by score on a financing knowledge test they administered. They found an almost perfect correlation between knowledge of financing and sales production. This seems to suggest that everybody wants to buy. Salespersons who can make the dream come true by finding effective financing solutions are the ones who make the sales. Interesting proposition. My bet is that this company operates in the first-time, lower-priced market. Even so, could this insight apply in your situation?

Personality, the final component of RUESAP, is in many respects the most powerful of all. It has to do with discovering the best ways to "connect" with individual prospects so the selling process moves more smoothly toward a successful close. The manner of communication style is an important issue here. If my very good friend and colleague, Charles Clarke III, MIRM, were here at this moment, he would chime in for his Bulls, Owls, Lambs, and Tigers™ (BOLT) program,[1] and he'd be very welcome to do so. The fact that I learned this material as the Social Style Grid[2] doesn't take away from BOLT at all. (For more about the Social Style Grid and BOLT, see chapter 9.) It is extremely valuable material in the behavioral side of psychology, and it is an absolutely indispensable portion of the body of sales techniques that must be mastered.

We have already mentioned and illustrated equally vital material from the motivational side of psychology, the Values and LifeStyles[3] typology from SRI International. Because it highlights motivation, VALS is the strongest material there is in determining *what* the gift is that prospects will buy. BOLT is the best material, in my judgment, for determining *how* to communicate that fact to prospects convincingly. The combination of the two is awesome in its power.

---

[1]Bulls, Owls, Lambs & Tigers, Charles Clarke III, MIRM, ©2004, Charles Clarke Consulting, Gainesville, GA 30503; 770-287-7808.

[2]The Social Style Grid, David Merrill and Roger Reid, ©1977, Wilson Learning Corporation, Edina, MN 55439; 800-328-7937.

[3]Values and Lifestyles (VALS) program, SRI International, 333 Ravenswood Avenue, Menlo Park, CA 94025; 650-859-5386.

Evaluate early
and never stop

The process of evaluating buying potential begins the instant you lay eyes on customers, and it only ends when they move into their new homes. You are always learning more about what makes them tick. But, the first cut at your professional evaluation should be completed before you leave the sales center. For many salespersons, the commitment to conduct a model tour is a commitment to spend 30 to 60 minutes or more with customers. It is easy for that to become even longer in large-scale master-planned communities where there are extensive recreational amenities to show. Salespersons who deal with these realities soon understand the value of conducting thorough prospect evaluations early.

Data dumping is a
sign of no training

At the other end of the professionalism scale are those untrained salespersons who don't want to know anything about their prospects. They act as though they feel it is their function to perform a data dump on prospects as they cross the model home threshold. "Welcome to XYZ Builders," they might say. "Is this your first time here?" If I say, "Yes." They will say something like, "Well, this is our Dogwood model. It has three bedrooms and two baths and contains nineteen hundred and eighty square feet of heated and cooled area. The fireplace you see in the living room is an extra, and the master bath tile is a designer upgrade. This home is $249,500 on a standard lot. This lot is $35,000 extra. The builder is offering $5,000 off for buyers who sign a contract this week. Do you need anything else, or can I sit back down?"

Well, maybe the question was a bit of a stretch, but what preceded it is absolutely typical. When I get dumped on like this, I generally respond by saying I just came in looking for a bathroom I can borrow for a moment. That generally quiets them right down. If I had indicated that I had been there before, I bet their response would have been, "Who did you work with?" This is at least a qualifying question, but I'm thinking the qualifying has more to do with who they'd have to split the commission with than it does with what I might already know.

Demonstrate

When you are satisfied that you have at least a first-level idea about a prospect's RUESAP profile, you deserve to decide whether to accompany them on a full-blown model and community tour. If traffic is slow and you have time, your standards might be lower than when traffic is high. That's understandable. The important thing is to set yourself up to make that decision and have a plan in mind for either eventuality.

"Why don't you folks get started in our Granville model, and I'll catch up with you in a few minutes," is a basic turn-away line. Another is, "Let me take just a moment to brief you on the highlights of our Granville model, and then you can take a look at it yourselves while I say 'Hello' to those folks over there who just arrived. Perhaps we will join you as you look around. Would that be all right with you?"

Build perceived product value

Once you commit to a demonstration of your product, your first goal is to build your customers' perception of value in the product you offer so that the price appears to be reasonable in comparison. The process followed is to ensure that the customer recognizes the value of everything in the product that costs the builder money to provide. This starts with an explanation of the desirable features and benefits of the surrounding area. Then, the presentation spirals inward to the community itself. Finally, the features and benefits of the dwellings themselves are presented in a manner designed to achieve maximum impact.

The underlying objective so far is to provide some reasonable justification of your finished homesite price. Most people cannot picture land value, but they're pretty good at judging structure values. If you paid too much for your land, you will have to skimp on the house to meet your price target. Customers will pick up on that right away and not like it.

Find the magic spot out front

Once your demonstration has spiraled down to the model home itself, be sure not to forget the exterior. It's common for the outside of a model home never to be demonstrated, because salespersons assume customers looked at it as they approached the door.

They didn't.

Every home has a "magic spot" somewhere out front from which the front elevation looks better than it does from any other spot. Go outside and look. Check out roof angles, columns, windows, the front door itself, your front stoop, the landscaping, etc. Walk around, watching some elements cover up and then reveal other elements until you get the most pleasing picture. When you do, you're standing on that home's magic spot. Hopefully, it is not out in the street, because you want to walk your customers to the front door every time, inviting them to stop for a moment while they're standing on the magic spot looking at the home.

Position customers on the magic spot

If you have a garage sales center and normally walk customers back outside so you enter the model through its front door (strongly recommended) make sure the walkway passes through the magic spot. When the three of you leave the sales center, make sure you go first in line with the prospect couple trailing behind. Walk through the magic spot and gracefully turn to face them as they step up to it. When you stop, they'll stop. They'll be standing on the magic spot, getting the best picture possible of that home's exterior, while you explain what they're looking at. You don't have to look at the home to describe it, so look at them looking at the home as you describe it. Remember, focus on the customer? Read in their faces and postures whether they like the home so far.

Use your judgment about how long to linger here. It's unlikely that you would stay more than a minute under the best of circumstances unless your customers ask a question. If the weather is unpleasant, 15 seconds might be your limit before turning toward the front door.

Back through the front door

Once inside, you are going to want to control where they go and how long they stay there. Trust me, you will. The way to make that happen is for you to approach the front door ahead of your prospects and take charge of opening it. When you get it open, step across the threshold while simultaneously turning to face them. Then back up however many steps it takes for you to get to the spot you've marked in your memory where you want to stop. You see, there is a magic spot in your entry foyer also that is the focal point for whatever magnetic appeal this home offers arriving guests. You want your customers to stand there for a moment as they form their first impression of the home.

Your cylinder of personal space

Your tool to make that happen is your cylinder of personal space. Stand up for a moment and extend your arms out to the sides, parallel to the floor. Now, spin around once without moving from the place you're standing. Your fingertips just described a circle in the air. Extend that circle down to the floor, in your mind, and you have made a cylinder. That is your cylinder of personal space. You carry it with you everywhere you go. Everybody else has their own cylinder, too. Managing these cylinders will be one of your strongest selling tools.

Here's the thing. Whenever circumstances permit, people who do not know each other very well like to keep their cylinders from overlapping. They become uncomfortable if they have to get any closer than two arm lengths away, your arm plus theirs.

Try it. When you stop in the foyer, they will want to stop no less than two arm lengths from you. So, you pick your stopping point so they can stop where they want to, and the spot they pick is exactly where you want them to stand to see the home's interior at its absolute best. Your architect sweated bullets to create this effect. Let them enjoy it for a moment and picture their guests arriving for dinner. They will never stand here again during your demonstration.

You may have to try this a couple of times before you get it just right, because there is the open front door to deal with. Usually, it works to ask one of them to close it for you.

Control where and when they move

This stuff is cool, folks. I am describing here a method whereby you can control exactly where customers walk as they view your model home. This gives you ultimate control over them. Do it right, and they'll never ever pick up on it. Every single decision they make about where they go will be one they make themselves to please themselves. Only you will know that what's really going on is that they are moving in response to your movements, so their cylinders of personal space are protected.

When I train salespersons to do this, I bring along a stack of paper plates. We number them one through about ten with a marker, and put number one outside where you stood to get them to stop on the magic spot. Number two might go just outside the front door, where you had to pause long enough to get it open. Number three can go in the foyer where you stopped after stepping through the doorway. Thereafter, we work out the exact sequence in which we would like to show the rest of the home, figuring where we would want prospects to walk and stand and then marking our resting spots to make it all happen. It's fun. We have lots of laughs figuring it out together.

Look at them looking
at your model home

In working out the sequence of standing spots for salespersons, try to observe several rules.

Try not to stop while standing in free space. Your cylinder eats up too much of the room and makes it feel smaller. Always try to stand next to a wall, so that half your cylinder is buried in it.

Never go into small rooms with prospects. Stay outside in the hallway.

You do not have to look at something in your model home to describe it to your customers. You've seen it before— thousands of times, most likely. It's much better for you to look at them while you describe it. Try to determine how they are reacting to the experience of being with you in this model home.

Resolve

Almost inevitably, the process of demonstration will be interrupted from time to time by customers asking questions or raising objections. Being able to answer these questions and resolve their objections without losing momentum is the hallmark of true sales professionalism. You have just got to know how to do this without becoming flustered. Not to worry. It really isn't too hard to handle objections if you have prepared yourself in advance.

Lots of material is available in other places for you to read about how to "handle" objections, so I'm planning to save some precious pages in this book by sparing you most of mine. However, I want to show you how to integrate some powerful body movements into the normal sequence of resolving objections.

First, move away and get small

As soon as you perceive an objection is being raised, it is a very good idea to adopt a thoughtful, nonthreatening body posture. Stepping back a bit is a good beginning, as is turning so you're standing with your body at something like a 45-degree angle relative to theirs. Tilting your head, and perhaps moving one hand to your chin area completes the pose. This body position is intended to make you appear smaller and less threatening to them, so they'll be encouraged to tell you more. Get real quiet and listen very carefully.

Everybody suggests asking clarifying questions and trying to restate their objection as a means for getting clearly in your mind what's going on in theirs. That's all good. If you think you're going to be involved in this phase for more than a few seconds, it is also good to come unstuck from your initial pose and begin to stroll about slowly. Take a looping track generally away from them as you focus on what's going on. It's okay to look away, as though you are deep in thought. Just maintain contact by meeting their eyes with yours from time to time.

It's hard in my experience for salespersons to do consistently better than the old "feel, felt, found" sequence. "I understand how you might *feel* that way. Others besides you have *felt* something similar. But, upon further examination they *found* that…their original objection was stupid." Oh, that isn't how that ends up? My bad.

Approach again and get powerful

As you formulate your response plan, you can start curving back toward them. Visualize the camera slowly zooming in on the president as he delivers an important thought from the Oval Office. That's what you are doing now as you approach the prospects head on with your body now squared with theirs. You are exerting the physical pressure of authority as you deliver your respectful response. If it seems appropriate to ask a tie-down question, you want to end up in the classic face-to-face, slightly off-balance, leaning-forward posture, okay? That was a tie-down question, wasn't it? I could ask another, couldn't I? You get the point, don't you?

Tie downs only work if the customer almost has to answer, "Yes" or you'll fall into them. Tie downs will fail almost every time if you do not have strong eye contact at the moment of asking. Even so, they are a great way to cement a positive response in the customer's head.

Select

When your customers begin to identify with your location, community, and product, it's time to select the one home that's perfect for them. This involves choosing the best design plan in the particular location they prefer. The idea is to create the feeling that there is one property only that best satisfies their needs and desires. Uniqueness fosters urgency. The fear of loss is the greatest aid to wrapping up the sale that there is. In fact, you cannot close until you have the force working for you.

Select is on the same "floor" in the little Building the Sale house as resolve is because I don't really know which one will come first. I'm sure they will both occur before you make the sale, but in which order I cannot say.

It's a treasure hunt— have fun with it

Of the two, select is probably more fun for most salespersons. It's a treasure hunt, a release for both of you, a chance to get out there, so to speak, and move around looking for exciting possibilities for the future.

Still, finding the *one* is vital. You cannot close on more than one home or homesite, so you have got to get there. When you do, a magic thing will happen in an instant: You will become all-powerful. When you started out, your customers had ultimate power over you. They did not have to buy a home at all, they didn't have to buy one today, and they didn't have to buy one from you. They could have walked away at any moment without losing anything, because there was nothing established in their minds yet that they wanted. The rules of the game command you to do all of the work, expending all of your energy without assurance they will do anything. All of that changes when they find the one.

Their fear of loss is your ultimate power

When they find the one, the power that was theirs flips to you in a heartbeat. Now, you can be the instrument of their getting the home they want, or you can sell it to somebody else. Urgency to buy springs up in front of them, and it will knock them over if they aren't careful.

I had this happen to me once. You know I'm a car nut, right? Well, there it was, late on a Saturday afternoon after a long day of car shopping. It was poised gracefully on the rotating turnstile in the center of the dealer's showroom. All the special lights like they have in jewelry stores were focused on it, making it gleam and sparkle. It was silver metallic all over with a black leather interior and really good rims. It even had a spoiler on the tail, and guess what? There was a line of bright red LEDs embedded in the spoiler that lit up when you pressed the brake pedal.

**Get away
from my car!**

I was done in an instant. It was *my* car. The salesman could hardly keep from laughing. I swear, he arranged for a string of new people to come in and admire that car and remark about the brake lights. They kept coming the whole time I was in the little room off to the side trying to get a good price. Man, was I urgent. Those other people were talking about buying *my* car.

What a lesson! When customers select the one, your power to relieve their anxiety is awesome. All you have to do is do it.

Close

This *is* the most important sales activity of all. Quite literally, if you cannot close, you cannot sell. Even so, all of us sometimes avoid closing because we instinctively fear rejection. We would rather ride home tonight thinking about our be-backs-for-sure than ask them to buy and be turned down. We worry about being pushy and driving them away. We fret about wanting to be nice and allow them space and time to decide without pressure. Besides, we are enjoying the emotional exhilaration of an imminent sale, and we just don't want to risk being smashed to the ground yet one more time.

Don't worry, all salespersons have been there. But, it doesn't have to be this way ever again. Avoiding this gut-churning moment is the whole idea behind the Building the Sale method. The fact that they are standing there with you is proof that you have done everything right, so far. By being with you, they are telling you they want to buy, and they're asking you to close the sale for them. Go for it!

Relax and close
with confidence

I am truly fond of spontaneous closing, where what comes next is whatever comes out of your mouth in the natural course of conversation. Remember, the idea of surrendering to spontaneity? When you know that you are a master of your selling technique and no longer have to think about it, you can just let go and let things happen. You will do whatever is right at exactly the right moment with what will seem like great skill, because you trust yourself to be totally in the moment instead of trying to plan ahead.

You have reason to feel confident at this moment. After all,

- You greeted these people warmly and made them feel welcome.
- You respectfully established control over the process you've been following with them.
- You identified their RUESAP and presented your products to answer their needs.
- You consciously built rapport with high touch.
- You demonstrated your product skillfully and established perceived value.
- You provided all necessary information in an organized, professional manner.
- You answered all their questions and resolved any objections there may have been.
- You encouraged choices and you found the "one."
- You allowed urgency to spring up and work for you.

It seems to me that you are on a roll, and closing should just happen. Still, I recognize that many salespersons would feel better if they had some examples to work from. So, here is a closing plan I like because it isn't as contrived as some are.

Try the new
Four-Step Close

If you like, you can call it the Four-Step Close. That's because it involves using four steps. They are

1. Confirm your prospects' choice.
2. Ask them to act.

3. Express your approval.
4. Deliver their gift.

1. **Confirm.** Use a simple statement or question to focus their attention on the fact that you've identified the one they want.

> "This home would be perfect for you, wouldn't it?"
> "Let's go ahead with this one, shall we?"
> "This one is your choice, isn't it?"
> "You are ready to decide now, aren't you?"

Notice, each of these examples is a tie-down question. There is no magic, but tie downs do encourage affirmative answers.

2. **Ask.** When they answer, ask them to take the next step.

> "Let me show you how to proceed, okay?"
> "Let's go do the paperwork, shall we?"
> "Why don't we go back to the office and tell them
>   this one is yours?"
> "How about we go handle the paperwork, all right?"

3. **Approve.** When they answer, express your approval.

> "Great!"
> "Wonderful!"
> "Congratulations!"
> "Fantastic!"

4. **Deliver** the gift.

> "You are going to be very happy here!"
> "Your friends will be green with envy!"
> "Your parents are going to be so proud!"
> "You are going to do very well with this home!"

Do you see how the gift statement changes? It is chosen by you to express in a nutshell what you've decided their special gift really is. This statement anchors their commitment to buy because the decision they just made is delivering its gift already. They are diving into the visualization dream you created for them, and you are in there too. It's time for all of you to enjoy it together!

For the Petersons in chapter four, the gift statement might have been, "You will cement a lot of important relationships in this home." For the Johnsons, a good one would have been, "Your children will really thank you for making this decision."

Follow-Up

Now, we come to the most underperformed activity in all of new home sales. Almost nobody does follow-up the right way. Oh, some salespersons do it some of the time for some of their prospects, but for most salespersons, it seems like follow-up is a really good idea they'll think about starting tomorrow.

No serious salesperson disputes the merits of doing follow-up. They easily see why it is depicted as it is in the Building the Sale diagram. Follow-up holds up however much of the sale you built today until the prospects come back for a return visit. Without follow-up, the "house" has only width and height. It is as thin as a sheet of paper standing on edge. It will start falling over as soon as you let it go when the prospects leave, unless you add the supporting third dimension of follow-up.

Would you like a 25% sales increase?

All salespersons understand the benefits of being able to follow-up effectively. However, some worry about being intrusive, and many dislike making follow-up telephone calls. For many salespersons, the market has been so strong for the past few years that follow-up just hasn't been necessary, even if they *could* find the time and energy to get it done. Still, from my experience with client companies that manage to get mobilized to do follow-up well, I have not yet seen one fail to increase their company-wide sales conversion ratio by less than 25%. Imagine what a 25% increase in your company's sales conversion ratio could mean! To begin with, it would probably allow you to cut back on expensive advertising, especially those ads you put in the newspaper each week.

The object of any good follow-up program is to maintain positive contact with your customers so that you can attract them to come back for another visit. Here is where the rapport you were able to create during the first visit will show its importance. By caring enough to stay in touch, you are showing your prospects that they are important enough to you to be remembered. Most people find that flattering.

Where does it say you can't visit?

There are four principal ways to conduct follow-up. The first is by dropping by for a personal visit at a prospect's home. Don't faint! It is not illegal to do this, just almost unheard of. What's wrong with taking by a small gift and leaving it with your card, or saying "Hello" briefly, if you get the chance? I'm not talking about going inside their house, unless asked. What I have in mind is a 20-second conversation at the front door. What an impression that makes.

The second method of conducting follow-up is with telephone calls. I am not in favor of intentionally leaving something out of your sales presentation so you have an excuse to call. That's phony. Besides, you don't need an excuse if you have a well-designed follow-up system. When we design follow-up plans, all scheduled calls make sense on their own so they'll be easier to make. Remember, nowadays, you need to be confident you have permission from your prospects to make follow-up calls.

The third method of providing follow-up is with individually crafted letters from salesperson to prospect. Doing these by hand would be wonderful, but for most salespersons this is utterly impossible. Having them drafted by a smart follow-up computer program is a much better idea. They can be personalized in startlingly wonderful ways so that prospects almost never figure out it is a computer writing to them.

The final method of delivering follow-up is with bulk mail drops. This method sends the same message to a large group of people all at once. Some builders use direct mail houses to help them manage such a program, and that's fine. Just be sure they don't use your names for other purposes. You owe your prospects their privacy.

Get follow-up done with smart software

The first secret to effective follow-up is to get purpose-written computer software to help you do the job. Our Prospect Action Control software has been helping builders and community developers do world-class follow-up for about 20 years. There are other excellent systems out there. Get somebody's software, and get busy.

The second secret is to put your effort where it will do the most good. That always means having a prospect classification system that is more realistic than "ready, willing, and able." I will devote a chapter later in this book to developing such a classification system. It has many benefits to offer you.

The third secret is to use automatically generated follow-up to encourage your salespersons to share all of their prospect information with you. Once you get complete and accurate information, you can begin making better decisions about a host of sales management issues.

Building the Sale Summary

Well, there you have it: a basic plan for organizing and delivering a powerful new home sales presentation depicted as a little house of dreams you make real for people one room at a time. As powerful as this approach to personal selling is, it cannot exist alone. It must be supported by what precedes your personal sales encounter and by what comes after. That's why the Building the Sale house rests on a homesite that depicts outreach, Internet, and delivery opportunities.

Attracting with Outreach

Outreach represents all those things you do to attract new prospects to your product offering, asking them in the process to consider it for themselves. Specific activities would include targeted advertising, public relations, on-site promotions, and Realtor relations. Until recently, something close to 100 percent of site-visiting prospects would have been attracted to you by your outreach activities and would have followed that approach to your welcome experience.

Adding the Internet

Many sales managers are coming to understand that over half of the prospects who visit their sales center have previously visited their company's web site. Many new home builders are discovering that their number one salesperson is the salesperson who handles Internet inquiries. Therefore, it just makes good sense to treat all sales center visitors like they are returning visitors, because it's highly likely that they are.

Pardon the play on words: They visited your site before coming to your site.

Assume all sales center visitors visited you first on the Internet

This reality just increases the value of welcoming sales center visitors warmly, like they are returning family members. From their perspective, they already have a relationship with your company, your community, your homes, and you, because they discovered you on the Internet and decided to spend some time with you there. In their hearts, they expect to be recognized and appreciated for taking that relationship to the next level: coming to see you in person.

Your company, your community, your homes, and you as a person enjoy celebrity status, because you are all media stars. No matter that the medium is only the Internet; you all appeared in color on the small bright screen. All of the psychological triggers that create celebrity have been pulled. Go with it!

Supporting with Delivery

No sales process can last for long or produce continuing sales unless it is supported by a robust delivery function. If you can't get the houses built right and delivered on time, your sales will soon dry up. That means every single person involved in your company's production activities holds a collateral position on your sales team. It's high time we recognize this and start pulling together like the team members we truly are.

By the same token, salespersons most often have their own roles to play in the delivery process. I am an advocate for restricting those activities to an absolute minimum, so as to free up salespersons' time and energy to concentrate on making more sales. Those jobs need to be done, however, by knowledgeable and caring individuals so that the chances of having them done well increase.

Going Even Farther

Keep in mind that Building the Sale, even when augmented by the Internet, is only the framework for organizing the presentation with basic skill sets that are needed to make it work. The sophisticated human communications material that will transform good salespersons into superstars is previewed for you in the next chapter. Come on, you'll love it!

CHAPTER NINE

Becoming a Sales
SUPERSTAR

T hree things you know about superstars: They're famous, they're the best at what they do, and they get paid a whole bunch of money.

What's less recognized about superstars is the gut-wrenching hard work they do behind the scenes. Athletes endure endless physical training, and many must overcome and play through painful injuries. Movie stars have to memorize lines and be in makeup before dawn for months on end. Both athletes and movie people must overcome the stark paralyzing fear of failure that precedes every performance. They risk public humiliation at any moment while reaching for fame and fortune. The fact that it's not easy at the top is proven by the number who turn to drugs, alcohol, or some other form of escapist behavior.

My dream for you is that you attain superstar status in new home sales, either as a salesperson, a sales manager, or as a home builder. Anybody want out? Now's the time to split if you're not ready to take this journey.

Fair enough. Remember back in chapter one, I mentioned the existence of a body of professional knowledge that applies to new home sales? So far, we have sketched out a vision of selling power that would be worth superstar incomes, and we have examined a sales presentation plan that can help you deliver that power to the selling process. Now, it is time to take a first look at the more advanced human understanding and communication components of that body of professional sales knowledge. It is in the mastery of these techniques that superstardom lives.

Nonverbal Communication

A great place to start is with the field of nonverbal communications, or body language. There are two major disciplines in the study of body language, and we have drawn from both of them already in this book. Both have complicated names, which I suppose are intended to lend an aura of academic legitimacy to them. Proxemics is the study of spacial relationships and personal territory. Mastering proxemics will help you understand how to move and where to stand during your sales presentation. Kinesics is the study of physical gestures and expressions and their possible meanings, so you'll have an idea what your customers are actually feeling and thinking, which may not agree with the words they are saying.

So far, we have drawn on proxemics to help guide customer movements during a model home demonstration and to shore up the effectiveness of tie-down questions when used to resolve customer objections. Proxemics also has a great deal to do with sales center design, which we will discuss in some detail in a later chapter.

Body movements reveal true feelings

The foundation of kinesics is that all of us employ gestures and postures in the course of communicating with others. Some of us develop a capability for saying things convincingly that we do not really mean or are simply not true. This can be troublesome for a salesperson trying to gauge how well the presentation is going. The study of kinesics reveals that very few people can conceal their true feelings in their gestures and postures. "The body doesn't lie," is a very useful insight in selling.

An example would be a couple, who we will shortly learn are *amiables*, who keep saying how much they like your home and how nice it is being with you, while crab-walking sideways toward the door. Amiable people really dislike conflict, so it is difficult for them to tell you that they don't like you or your model. They can't hide the truth, though, that their bodies are revealing. The fact of the matter is that they can't wait to get away, so they are edging toward the door.

What do crossed
arms mean?

Almost everyone would say that arms crossed over someone's chest is a sign that the person is closed or resistant to the idea being discussed. This is a common misconception based on an incomplete understanding of kinesics. The truth may be that this person customarily adopts this pose as a matter of physical comfort and it has nothing to do with their attitude. It is, in fact, the *transition into or out of a pose* that has special meaning. If a person has been walking around with their arms and hands freely moving and then goes into the arms-over-chest pose when the price of your home comes up, that would be a sign that the price may be a problem for them.

One of the big factors that separates accomplished actors from the rest of us is their ability to control their postures and gestures consciously. Just for fun some evening, turn off the sound on your favorite TV sitcom or drama and watch the actors' body language. I bet you'll soon see you don't even need the sound to understand exactly what is going on.

Rely on
body clues

For regular folks, you would do well to watch for body language clues. If there is a conflict between what they are saying verbally and what their body is telling you, go with the body.

Here's a last thought on body language before we move on. Entire books have been written on this subject, many with semilurid covers promising dating help inside. When you read them, you are more likely to find a finely detailed research project report with all the relevance of rats exploring mazes. They're truly awful, take it from me. Kinesics is extremely powerful in a much simpler package. It all boils down to whether your customers are expressing approval or disapproval in their gestures. Learning how to read these signs is a critically important element in our body of professional sales knowledge.

Behavioral Typologies

Next, I would recommend mastery of the Social Style Grid[1]; Bulls, Owls, Lambs and Tigers™ (BOLT)[2]; DISC[3]; or even Myers-Briggs[4] as your key to understanding how to communicate with your customers. Many of you who have been to a BOLT presentation may be tempted to think you've already gotten it and that it is now "old hat." Not so, I bet. Knowing that it exists is a victory, for sure, but until you have mastered it, BOLT cannot serve you in your profession.

Knowing Cessna and Piper make private aircraft is a nice piece of knowledge to have, but it doesn't qualify you to fly one. The same is true of whichever behavioral typology you choose.

Pick the system you like, and then really get into it, okay? They all have a lot in common. It's a matter of judging two dimensions of observable behavior in your prospects, drawing a conclusion from your observation of their preferred communicating style, and then adapting your normal style to fit theirs more closely. The result is that communication between you will go much more smoothly, and they will think of you as "their kind" of person.

Observe assertiveness and responsiveness

The two dimensions of behavior to look for are assertiveness and responsiveness. Assertiveness refers to how willful individuals appear to be in influencing the actions of other people. Assertive people come on strong, with direct statements and instructions. Less assertive people tend to be more laid back. They ask and suggest when they want something.

---

[1] The Social Style Grid, David Merrill and Roger Reid, ©1977, Wilson Learning Corporation, Edina, MN 55439; 800-328-7937.

[2] Bulls, Owls, Lambs & Tigers, Charles Clarke III, MIRM, ©2004, Charles Clarke Consulting, Gainesville, GA 30503; 770-287-7808.

[3] DISC Personal Profile System, John Geier, ©1977, Performax Systems International.

[4] Myers-Briggs Type Indicator, Peter B. Myers & Katherine D. Briggs, ©1980, Consulting Psychologists Press, Inc., Mountain View, CA 94043; 800-624-1765.

As with responsiveness, there is no preferred place to be on the assertiveness scale. This is sometimes hard for sales types to accept, because we're all wedded to the idea of the in-your-face sales ideal. Validated research indicates, however, that there are just as many successful salespersons who are less assertive as there are more assertive ones. It's just a matter of how they prefer to get the job done.

The responsiveness dimension is a measure of the degree to which individuals allow you to see their inner feelings and emotions. More responsive individuals light up with movements, gestures, expressions, and voice emphasis to make it quite clear how they feel. Less responsive people tend to damp down their feelings and emotions, so it's harder to see what's going on inside.

Here's a diagram that will help you sort this all out. In this particular picture, assertiveness is measured on the horizontal scale, and responsiveness is depicted on the vertical scale. Note how the intersection of the two creates four possible preferred styles of communicating.

There are generally four communication styles as shown here. We know from research that *expressive* people prefer a fast-paced, highly energized presentation that focuses on dreams for the future. *Drivers*, however, want the presentation to move quickly—because time is money—and they would like to stick to business and get it done. *Analytical* individuals want to be more deliberate in pace and focus strictly on facts and figures. They are wary of sales hype, and they need time and space to draw their own conclusions. *Amiables*, on the other hand, want to go slowly on real estate and take lots of breaks for personal stuff. The whole idea of a receiving a sales presentation and being asked to make a decision is stressful to amiables.

Prepare four distinct
sales presentations

You can see that this information suggests that salespersons should have four basic presentations ready to go that differ in content, energy, and pace. In my world, before they step away from the site plan display in your sales center, all salespersons would have made a decision about which presentation to deliver. Not that they cannot change their minds and modify their approach as they go along, but at least they should have made a specific decision about how to start.

The particulars of each of the typologies mentioned here differ somewhat, but the basics are the same. You measure specific parameters, and you decide which of the four types you are dealing with. On the basis of your judgment, each would suggest specific things salespersons should do to make a better connection with their prospects.

Oh, the folks at Myers-Briggs would probably take exception. They maintain they measure four parameters and depict them on four horizontal lines. In my judgment, it makes no real difference. It's all the same stuff. So, grab whichever one floats your boat and master it. Because Charles Clarke III, MIRM, is one of us, I'd favor your getting in touch with him.

Consumer Psychographics

Now you'll be ready to move into consumer psychographics. Building on observable behavior, which gives you communication clues, psychographics deals with the inner motivations, which we know by experiment govern consumer purchasing decisions. People buy things that bring them a reward beyond the utility of the product itself. Understanding how different people define the rewards they want is the key to the bank in new home sales. If it occurs to you now that this might be the basis of our discussion of the gift in chapter two, you're absolutely right.

Here's an example that illustrates positioning products to deliver emotional rewards. Picture in your mind, please, an image of a male person in his thirties, on his way home from work in the afternoon, standing in a store, reaching out and picking up a six pack . . . of Pabst Blue Ribbon beer. Can you see this person? What is this person wearing?

Hundreds of groups I've spoken to spontaneously say that this guy is wearing a work shirt, jeans, and boots. They say he takes his Pabst outside, jumps into his pickup truck, and drives away.

From my point of view, they are exactly right in their depiction of this person. I hope you came close. You are now halfway through the exercise. Bear with me another moment, please, so we can finish up. Wipe that image out of your mind, and we will proceed to form a new one.

Now picture in your mind an image of a male person in his thirties, on his way home from work in the afternoon, standing in a store, reaching out and picking up a six pack . . . of Heineken beer. Can you see this person? What is this person wearing?

Again, hundreds of audiences have said this person is wearing a dress shirt, perhaps with a loosened tie, and suit pants. They say he takes his beer outside, jumps into his BMW, and drives away.

I hope you saw these guys as well as audiences have, because getting this picture means you get the message of brand positioning. In my opinion, beer is much closer to being a true commodity than new houses are. I'm sure there are individuals out there who would argue with me vigorously, but, hey, all beer is wet and cold, all beer is some shade of yellow/brown, all beer is foamy, and all beer tastes bitter and yeasty. I don't care where the water comes from, it is all purified anyway before it goes in the vat. Besides, as we have discussed, all wheat is pretty much wheat, all barley is barley, and all hops are hops. Across the spectrum, beer is what, 98% the same?

Yet, brewers have spent billions of dollars convincing us that beers are not the same. There was once a national campaign that suggested their beer was better because it was colder! What could possibly have been up with that?

**We buy psychic
gratification**

Why did the first guy pick up the Pabst and the second guy pick up the Heineken? Most folks first suggest that price was a factor, so let's look at that one. In most parts of the country, Heineken would be close to twice as expensive as Pabst, but the real difference would be 3 or 4 dollars. If the first guy was planning on buying a six pack a day, that could become a problem. If he had decided he wanted the Heineken tonight, he could have bought it, but he didn't. Why? It turns out that positioning is the answer.

You see, for years and years—decades even—Pabst Blue Ribbon has been positioned in advertising as the brand of choice for red-blooded, what-you-see-is-what-you-get, a-day's-work-for-a-day's pay, solid, dependable American working males. Heineken, on the other hand has long been promoted with the line, "Someday, you can have the best of everything. Tonight, you can have the best beer in the world. You can have a Heineken."

The next question is, Who is prouder of his choice, the Pabst drinker, or the Heineken guy? Who do you think?

The real answer is that this is a trick question. They are both proud of their choice, because they are both proud of who they are. There is honor and nobility in leaving something tangible behind after a day's labor. You better believe those guys are proud of their ability to endure tough working conditions and get the job done. The number of pickup trucks you see on the road is a good indicator of that. The other guy is equally proud of the fact that he is a "fast mover," on the way up toward a bright future based on brains and ambition. He hopes all the rest of us notice his beer selection, because if we do, we'll get the message and be impressed.

Gratification is the gift

I hope the connection between psychographic positioning and the gift is crystal clear. Both beer buyers bought a gift. The first guy's gift was something like, "I'm rough. I'm tough. I know what I'm doing, and I get the job done. You girlie boys couldn't last a day with me." The other guy's gift is, "I'm working hard and working smart to get ahead. I'm moving on up and getting ready to score big time. You clods better take notice. I'm coming through."

Now, maybe you believe their gift represents the reality of their lives, or perhaps you believe that it is a fantasy of what they *wish* their lives were like. Perhaps each of us has a message we tell ourselves is the truth and another message that we suspect is the truth. We buy products whose brand image resonates with what we wish in our secret hearts were true about us. In the buying, we make our dream selves seem more real.

Maybe that's why pickup trucks have huge grills and are pictured in larger-than-life scale dominating the wilderness in TV ads. That may be the fantasy of those who buy them: that they could really be powerful, independent, and in control, masters of their destiny, totally self-reliant, doing what they please when they please, and answering to no one but themselves.

Is this deep enough for you, yet? If you're spinning a bit, take a moment. This is worth getting. This can change your professional life.

This is how it's done

I promise you this is how big-time marketing is done. People who spend millions on national ad campaigns do not mess around. They intend to touch their target buyers in secret ways with hidden messages that cause action. It's not important to them whether their customers understand. It's only important that their customers react and buy.

All of this is great news for home-building companies. We can position ourselves and our products with relative ease using these techniques. Now that you've been clued in, I have to ask you a very interesting question. Will you do anything about this in your company, or will you let it pass you by?

Are you ready?

Please, pick up this ball and run with it. To begin with, look around at your competition. In almost every market, there is at least one builder whose position is based on solid craftsmanship, honest dealing, and customer satisfaction. Correspondingly, if you have people like our Heineken drinker in your market, there is almost certainly a builder of charismatic homes chosen by people because those homes make a statement about the people who own them.

What's likely at work in these instances is that principals of many building companies pick out a market position that resonates with how they view themselves. In fact, they probably don't look upon it as positioning at all. They are just doing what comes naturally.

The new idea I am proposing here is setting out on purpose to discover a position that resonates with a promising segment of the home-buying public and then developing strong identity in that position as a basis for your whole marketing strategy. I promise you this can be done to great advantage for home builders. I have devoted more than 20 years of my professional life to learning how to do this.

Although we may be discussing psychographic positioning here as a marketing concept, we're only doing it this way to set up salespersons and their managers to use these concepts with prospects they meet. Psychographic positioning works best when building companies go at it with purpose-designed homes, purpose-crafted ads, targeted model merchandising, and sales presentations that wrap it all together. This is truly the inside track to inducing people to line up to pay a premium to own one of your homes.

**Builders take heed
and make money**

At this level, your business success has little to do with lumber and drywall prices. You're playing a different game now, where the potentials for profit are much greater. You are engaged in the *home selling* business, not the home building business. Life is sweet here as your margins and shares grow.

Negotiation Skills

Negotiation skills are another essential tool that will serve you well in making winning sales presentations. There is a wealth of material to use that was originally developed for the folks who live in the crucible of manufacturer's rep versus purchasing agent in industries outside the home-building business. You see, in this setting, the rep wants to sell his products at the highest possible price, with the most relaxed specs and with the most liberal delivery and service requirements. The purchasing agent wants just the opposite in each parameter of the sale. Isn't it easy to see that one must win and the other must lose? This leads lots of people to think pretty hard about how to tilt the odds of success in one direction or the other.

We can make excellent use of their ideas, because a sales presentation is really a funny sort of negotiation. Many of the same principles apply. In the study of negotiation techniques, developing an understanding of power, where it comes from, and how to use it is essential.

Among the classic sources of power in negotiation are the following:

Alternative Power	This is the freedom to walk away without doing business unless the business pleases you.
Expertise Power	The person who knows more about the subject being discussed has the advantage.
Position Power	Having the home field advantage, doing business on your turf, gives you the confidence edge.
Print Power	Anything printed must be policy from higher authority and thus isharder to change.
Commitment Power	We all respect a skillful, loyal advocate of their position, even if we don't agree.
Identification Power	We would prefer to do businesswith someone we like, rewarding them for their niceness.
Investment Power	The more time and effort we devote to a deal, the more we want it to work.
Information Power	The person who knows more about the other person's needs has a definite edge.
Reward Power	The person who can reward or punish the other has a big advantage.
Coercive Power	The person who can force the other to perform doesn't need to negotiate.

If the deal is that the person who gets more power sources on their side wins, then we should be very happy in the new home sales business. Because of the way we operate, we start out with seven of the ten power sources. We know more about buying and selling homes, so we have expertise power. We do business in our sales center and model home, so we have position power. We print our specs, prices, and contracts, so we have print power. We are *always loyal* to our builder principal, so we have commitment power. We work hard to build rapport with customers, so we have identification power. We are willing to spend time making the deal work, so we have investment power. We get to ask qualifying questions of prospects, so we have information power.

We have to throw out coercive power in our business, because nobody can force anybody to do anything in buying or selling new homes. This means that we start out with seven of nine power sources on our side.

The challenge is that the two power sources our customers have are big. They start out with alternative power, as we discussed in chapter eight. When you first meet prospects, they do not have to buy a home. They do not have to buy a home today. They do not have to buy a home from you today. They have alternative power. They can walk away at any time, because they have nothing to lose.

Also, when you first meet prospects, they have reward or punishment power. They can reward you by buying a home from you, or they can punish you by not buying.

You can close with confidence

When you help customers find the one they want, the reason you can close with confidence is that both of the powers they had before jump over to you. Now, you have alternative power: You can sell the home to them, or you can sell it to somebody else (like I thought that auto dealer was going to do). You also get reward or punishment power on your side: You can reward them by helping them buy the home they want, or you can punish them by taking it away.

Whenever you encounter salespersons who are discouraged by the number of sales they are not making, share this negotiation material with them. There is absolutely no reason for salespersons in our business to feel powerless over customers. Quite the opposite is true. We start off in a great position. If you just follow the Building the Sale method, you will arrive at the point of closing with the final two power sources in your control. How can you lose?

Neurolinguistic Programming

Neurolinguistic programming (NLP) is another body of knowledge that I have found to be essential for superstar salespersons. After all, the *ability to persuade* customers is the mark of your value as a salesperson, and it's what builders assume you're doing now. If you really want to know how to persuade someone, the answers you seek will be found in NLP. I promise you, it will be worth the effort.

Visualization is programming yourself for peak performance

Visualization is an NLP technique that is becoming more and more familiar to people through its importance in sports psychology. The idea is to visualize yourself doing all the things you need to do to be successful—actually seeing yourself doing them, and actually seeing the success you desire taking place—all in your mind's eye. Perhaps you've seen the Olympic downhill racer, standing at the top of the course, swaying back and forth before approaching the starting gate. That skier is seeing the course that lies below and is moving mentally through each gate, programming the body, as it were, to do the required moves with minimum loss of time.

As a speaker, I promise you that I visualize every presentation I make before entering the hall. I may not see the whole thing, because I always want to be spontaneous, but I certainly see pieces of the speech, and I work out specific wordings that seem to connect with the audience in my head.

That is the usefulness I see in visualization for salespersons. Each day, before making your first presentation, it would be a great idea for you to run through a successful one in your head. Maybe that means you get to the sales center a bit early. Maybe that means you don't listen to the local shock jocks on the radio while driving to work. However you get it done, visualizing yourself making successful presentations to happy home buyers will do a lot to increase your selling power.

Make contact, then lead

Mirroring is an NLP technique that suggests you should try to match your prospects' movements, voice level, and pace of speaking as a means of building confidence and rapport. You can overdo this, but the idea is to watch your prospects closely and do what they do, a few seconds later. If one touches her head as she puzzles over a question you asked, you touch your head also. Mirroring often happens spontaneously. Haven't you ever been sitting at a table across from someone in a meeting when suddenly the other person leans back and stretches? Pretty soon, someone else at the table will do the same thing, maybe even you.

Once you establish contact through mirroring, the NLP concept is that you can begin to lead the other person through the power of your influence. It's not that you want them to scratch their heads when you scratch yours, rather it's that you want them to accept your advice when you suggest that the home you want to sell them is the one they ought to buy.

Looking Toward Mastery

We have now looked at five separate components of the body of professional knowledge that I think defines new home sales. It is a substantial body of knowledge to master, but isn't the point to aim for superstardom? If you want to reach the top, you have to be worthy. It isn't an impossible mountain to climb. You've already started. From now on, you'll just get better and better as you accumulate knowledge in each of these fields.

If you'd like some help, sing out. I'm here, and I know these ideas work.

CHAPTER TEN

Organizing Prospect
MANAGEMENT

So far in our journey together, we have covered seven chapters that describe a vision of remarkable power in new home sales—the sort of selling power that would command both respect and high compensation. I refuse to believe that salespersons in our business cannot operate at this level. Then in chapter eight, I outlined a method for organizing an effective new home sales presentation. Chapter nine presented a synopsis of human relationship and communication material that I think salespersons should master if they aspire to operate at the levels we describe in this book.

Now, the time has come for me to share some practical thoughts about how to get organized to lead salespersons to greatness. If you are a sales manager or a building company principal, the next few chapters in this book will help you take specific steps toward solid improvements in performance. If you are a motivated salesperson, bring these ideas to your manager and volunteer to help get them implemented. You'll be building your career success in the process.

Most Valuable Asset

Let's start the discussion of prospect management with the assertion that prospects are the most valuable assets any home building company has. Prospects represent future sales, and as I have established, there is no reason to build houses if no houses are being sold. As painful as it might be for some of our friends who actually do the building to accept, their jobs and the paychecks that feed their families depend absolutely on the ability of salespersons to sell houses.

That's why it is so astonishing to me how poorly most building companies manage their prospect assets. Every building company counts its cash assets. Every building company inventories its physical assets. How come so many building companies have no clue about their prospects?

Several possible reasons occur to me, none of which I find acceptable. I have already alluded to the unfortunate fact that many builders feel out-of-their-depth when the subject shifts to marketing and sales. They prefer to stay with stick and brick issues that are within their comfort zone. I promise, there is no need for builders to feel that way, and I hope you don't know any who do.

Root out secrecy and superstition

Another reason for this incredible circumstance is that a combination of secrecy and superstition has been allowed to become a paradigm in new home sales. Just look like you're going to pick up a salesperson's card file of prospects, and you'll have a real unhappy camper on your hands in a heartbeat.

"Those are *my* people," you're likely to hear. "Don't you be messing with any of them. If I ever leave here, I'm gonna call every one of them and sell them a house. 'Course, as long as I'm here, I'm not planning to call *any* of them, but if I ever leave, you just watch out!"

I'm kidding, of course (sort of).

I can understand the superstitious hankering not to put the kibosh on an upcoming sale by telling the boss about it. I can also understand not wanting anyone in the company to know you just had a hot one in, because then they're going to expect you to make the sale. The trouble is that we have allowed these natural feelings to take control and dictate the way we operate. This cannot continue. If it is up to you, you have to stop this.

Prospects Belong to the Company

First, prospects belong to the company. The company spends large amounts of money to attract them. The company entrusts them to salespersons for handling. When sales are made, the company pays the salespersons the full commission due, without deducting the costs of producing the prospects who bought. Prospects belong to the company and are lent, free of charge, to salespersons.

How many prospects would you like to buy?

Sometime, just for fun, start a sales meeting by asking salespersons how many prospects they'd like to buy from you this coming week. You can offer to sell them at your cost, no mark-up involved. See how many takers you get.

The Company Has a Right to Know

Next, the company has the right to find out about their inventory of prospects. Salespersons simply must share that knowledge. If they balk, they leave. It's as simple as that.

You see, the real reason they don't want you to see their prospect records is that they are ashamed of their prospect records. Sooner or later, you will have to deal with that.

Start with Traffic Reporting

I have often found in severe cases that a good way to get control is to establish a reasonably good weekly traffic reporting system. Then, after a level of trust builds up, you can raise the issue of previously existing prospects.

Weekly traffic reports are mandatory

Every sales center should submit a weekly report of traffic. The very most basic report would ask for a count of first-time visitors and a count of return visitors by day of the week. Monday is probably the most popular reporting day, because it gets weekend traffic into the system right away. The next step in sophistication would be to account for which salesperson handled which visitors, if you have more than one salesperson.

Demand Truth

You must establish in your relationship with reporting salespersons that you expect the truth in traffic reporting—the absolute truth. Make sure they realize that nothing that is the truth will ever be used to harm a salesperson, but a lie will cause their swift dismissal. You cannot manage a business with garbage information. All of your decisions will be wrong.

There's another, deeper reason for demanding the truth. Every time a salesperson submits an untrue traffic report, they take a little chunk out of their body of self-worth. Every time their manager accepts an untrue report, knowing it is likely untrue, the manager loses a little chunk of self-worth also. How can this be any good?

For either to be effective, the channel of communication and mutual support must be open. It's the manager's responsibility to make sure this happens.

Provide Respect

A good way to open the channels of communication and support is to assure salespersons that they are appreciated and respected. The underlying reason they are sometimes tempted to falsify traffic reports is that they fear something bad will happen to them if they tell the truth. You will be miles ahead if you dispel that notion. There is no problem in real estate sales that we cannot solve if we just know about it. It's the ones you don't know about that eat your lunch.

Sales Conversion Ratio

Salespersons are often concerned about their sales conversion ratio, the number of prospects on average they must see to make a sale. There are two ways for salespersons to improve their sales conversion ratios. One is to sell more homes, which is good but difficult. The other way is to register fewer prospects. This is easy, especially if they are alone in the sales center.

**Remove the
pressure to lie**

My personal belief is that most salespersons don't intend to out-and-out lie when they decide not to count somebody. They just find ways to justify not calling a visitor a prospect. "Well you know, she had red hair. We've never sold to a redhead—probably never will. She's not a real prospect. It wouldn't be right to count her."

Grant Amnesty

My heartfelt recommendation is that you tell your salespersons you will never use sales conversion ratios to compare individual performance again. You stand to gain such huge value in truthful traffic reporting that it should be easy for you to make this concession.

**Sales conversion
ratios are suspect**

Sales conversion ratios were never a very good sales management tool anyway. There are way too many variables, some unmeasurable and others beyond the control of salespersons, that affect sales conversion ratios. Only when comparing salespersons working side by side in a single sales center over a long period do sales conversion ratios have any possible validity, and having sales centers staffed that intensely is not the operating mode for most builders. So why not just give them up and get something much better in return?

Encourage Prospect Grading

Grading prospects is a very good idea, in my judgment. It is the next step in traffic reporting beyond simply counting. It asks salespersons to share their overall feeling about each prospect's buying potential using a simple coding system anybody can understand. The basic idea, of course, is to add a measure of quality to the count of traffic coming through your sales center. Both quality and count are good leading indicators of sales to come.

There is a tradition in new home sales to grade prospects on a ready-willing-able system. The best prospects are judged to be ready, willing, and able. Medium-quality prospects have two of the three factors in place. Poor prospects have only one going for them.

I must confess that I have never understood this system. Let me ask you: If a prospect is ready, willing, and able, where's the contract? If there is no contract, then doesn't that mean the prospect is short, somehow, in at least one of those measures?

Rather than argue about it, allow me, please, to propose another grading system that I think both managers and salespersons will like better. It has more than three categories, which provides more flexibility for salespersons to describe their site-visiting prospects. It also includes two new categories that will allow salespersons to take themselves off the hook of describing all prospects as buyers. You are free to adjust all specifics of category definitions to suit your situation better. This is just a prototype to get you started.

A   Excited by what they saw. Fully qualified. We discussed it. May have picked a favorite. Expect them to buy something like what we showed them from somebody like us within 10 days.

B   Liked what they saw a lot, but are still evaluating an alternative we discussed, or are not yet quite sure what they want. Fully qualified. Will likely decide to buy something within 30 days.

C   Motivated shoppers. Apparently qualified. Like what we have, but they have more work to do. More than 30 days, less than 180 from making a buying decision.

D   Early in their shopping. Urgency is softer. Not sure exactly what will work for them. Dreaming as well as shopping. More than 6 months, less than 18 months from buying.

E   They were here and registered. We were working with other prospects, so we were not able to make a thorough evaluation. Invite them back.

F   Unlikely to buy from us. Serious disconnects exist between what they want and what we have. Perhaps not qualified at all.

These categories apply to site-visiting prospects who actually cross your threshold. You could have other categories for non–site-visiting prospects if you like, for telephone inquirers, reader service card re-turnees, Internet visitors, etc.

About Those E and F Prospects

Both of these eventualities happen in real life. You are far better off to get them counted than to have them remain hidden. Dealing with them is a mark of a good traffic-reporting system.

Deal with reality

Weekends produce most of the E prospects, but they can happen anytime. If too many of them occur, management will have to do something to remedy the situation. Salespersons reflexively think you'll put on another salesperson, thereby cutting their compensation potential on the slice-of-pie principle. They need to understand that adding another salesperson is probably management's last alternative. Even if it were to occur, it would not affect the original salesperson's annual income this year, or any other year. There will always be more homes to sell.

Nonprospects do visit you

A mark of respect for salespersons comes in allowing them to qualify site visitors as nonprospects. Professional salespersons meet and evaluate nonprospects every day. The ready-willing-able system does not recognize them, so they either get miscategorized or they go uncounted. This is easy to fix.

No Second Guessing

A recommended feature for the traffic-reporting system we're constructing here is that there will be no second guessing of salespersons' prospect ratings. Who would be in a better position to evaluate prospects than your salespersons who worked with them?

Even so, experience teaches that salespersons develop curious rating habits that you will need to be aware of. Some salespersons love everybody. They will have a disproportionate number of highly rated prospects. Other salespersons prefer to understate traffic quality, so that when they make a sale, it looks like they worked a miracle. Take these human foibles with a smile, and remember, over time, every salesperson's traffic will be the same. It's always a bell-shaped curve if your sample is big enough. A few great people come in, and a few toads show up. Mostly, it's folks in the middle.

Use the differences in rating averages that show up in your staff to trigger meaningful counseling. It's not to say they're doing something wrong, it's to help them do even better. Be extremely careful not to set rating expectations too strongly. Once salespersons get a clue what they're supposed to report, they will start making your expectations come true.

I once came across a very impressive sales manager who was especially proud of her detailed statistical records of traffic evaluations and sales conversion. Over five years, or so, with thousands of traffic units per year, her staff's evaluations and conversions hadn't varied by more than a few tenths of one percent from year to year. Her view was that this meant her traffic-reporting system was functioning well. Was it?

Prospect Registration Forms

It seems customary in our business to use some form of guest registration to record a prospect's visit. We could devote an entire book to this subject, but let's not, okay? A few highlights would be good to include in our discussion of prospect management because the registration form you use sets the stage for everything that follows.

Where did your form come from?

First, let's deal with the form you are using now. Unless you are extremely unusual, your form was copied from Sally's form down the road. Sally got her form from Jose, who got his from Tom, who got his from Fred, who was clueless to begin with.

Please consider starting all over with a clean sheet of paper. Decide what you would really like to know about prospects that would significantly change what you do with them while you're together. If you don't intend to do anything with the answers you get, don't ask the questions. You pay a price for each piece of information in terms of prospect aggravation. Use high touch: Keep your intrusion to a minimum.

Also, consider postponing the use of the form until later in your time with prospects. After they have become comfortable with you, they will give you much better answers. Asking them to fill out the card before you talk to them is high tech, impolite, and off-putting.

The Great Source Question

I will bet that one of the questions on the registration form you borrowed from somebody else has to do with the advertising exposure the prospects saw that triggered their visit to you. First, if the multiple-choice answers you provide include "Driving By," my bet is that one accounts for about 85% of your responses. Prospects normally don't want to reveal the level of interest they may have in your product too early, so they will naturally choose the acceptable answer that shows the least commitment on their part. It's not a lie. They were driving by. It's just a nonanswer. It doesn't tell you anything you didn't already know. Get rid of it.

**Why do you
want to know?**

Next, ask yourself why you ask this question at all. Do you really tally up all the responses you get in a year's time and use them to govern your advertising expenditures? If not, drop the question. Besides, don't you really know where you need to spend your money in your market already?

Ultimate Prospect Management

So far in this discussion of prospect management, I have been describing a system based on paper forms and reports. Ultimately, you may want to shift to a computer-supported system. When you do, my suggestion is that you purchase a purpose-written new home sales management software package. There are several good ones to choose from. Our Prospect Action Control (PAC) software system is one of them.

**Effective follow-up
is computer dependent**

Any of these systems will offer instant benefits. The first is that you gain access to prospect files. No longer will it be possible for salespersons to hide them away in metal file boxes. That alone will improve the quality of information that is recorded about your prospect inventory. The second benefit is that any of these software systems will draw upon individual prospect records to compile a large number of useful management reports. As long as salespersons share their individual prospect records with the system, it will no longer be possible for them to edit management reports to make them look better.

Provide a powerful incentive to share

How to you get salespersons to share their prospect records with the computer? The answer we've found in the PAC system is by giving them something in return that is immensely valuable and unobtainable by any other means: automatically generated personalized follow-up. In PAC, each prospect rating category has attached to it a preplanned stream of follow-up contacts appropriate in content and timing to people in that category, as defined earlier in this chapter. PAC prepares each follow-up contact using personal information it finds in each prospect's record, so that each person receives individualized follow-up. The richer the information stored in each prospect's file, the richer the personalization the computer applies to their follow-up.

The idea is to encourage salespersons to learn more about their prospects, because they will get a return on their investment in the quality of follow-up produced on their behalf. This is the ultimate use of high tech to produce the human warmth of high touch. It really works.

CHAPTER ELEVEN

Providing Reasonable Sales
FACILITIES

N ow that we have a handle on prospect management, let's turn our attention to the subject of providing reasonable sales facilities for your sales staff to use.

A Sales Center, Please

You cannot hope for salespersons to perform well if you set them up to meet prospects at the front door of your model home. You must provide some sort of sales facility that prospects are drawn to before they are granted access to the model.

Remember the story about playing Jai-Alai rather than baseball? Salespersons require time and space to get to know prospects—to learn about their RUESAP profiles—before commencing demonstrations of your new homes. The most common sales facility in use by new home building companies is the garage attached to the model home. I feel so strongly that this is a good idea that I am comfortable in making the following offer. If your budget for sales is so constrained that all you can afford to do in providing a sales center is to sweep out the garage, install a card table with a few chairs, and open the door on weekends, do it!

Please, please do not set your salespersons up in the front bedroom of the home, or worse still, in a back bedroom where they can't see prospects as they arrive. You cannot hope to even approach your maximum selling potential if this is your mode of operation.

Back-of-Heads Salesmanship

When you meet prospects at the front door, you will be giving them access to what they want to see without getting anything in return. The salesperson will be nothing more than a bother at this point. Prospects will steam right by and only show your salesperson the backs of their heads as they move about the home.

**You break right,
I'll break left**

If they are experienced shoppers, the prospects will split to make things even more confusing. The wife will break left, and the husband will break right. Maybe they'll cross in the family room. Maybe they will only meet again at the front door on their way out. Any salespersons placed in that position will be standing by helplessly, hoping that an opportunity will arise to inject themselves into the process. That opportunity may never come.

Site Plan Table Display

If your budget will allow something more than the swept-out garage, please make your next investment one of providing some sort of community site plan to place on the card table. Prospects need something to look at when they first come in your facility. A horizontal site plan display is a natural to capture their attention. If you can only afford the very basic, get a blue print of the community. The next step up would be to have an artist color it with markers. Put a clear plastic covering over it to protect it from coffee stains, and you will have created a nifty writing surface to boot.

Shop around a bit, and you'll discover that folks can figure out how to spend $50,000, or more, on a display like this. That's grand by me, but the function doesn't get any better this way, and it's the function that counts.

**Salespersons need
a chance to look**

Salespersons need an opportunity early in the presentation to look their prospects over. Trust me, you *can* tell a lot about a book by its cover. What we want salespersons to look for is that newly arriving prospects have some reasonable degree of similarity to folks you've been successful in selling to. This has nothing to so with race, ethnicity, or any other protected status. It has partly to do with whether these folks look like they could afford to buy one of your homes. For example, casual dress is fine. Tattered and torn casual dress is suspect, Britney Spears notwithstanding. Soiled clothing is a dead giveaway.

Salespersons can also get a good glimpse into psychographic profile by conducting such an inventory. Figure that each person dressed on purpose to deliver a certain message before leaving home this morning. What do you suppose the message might be? Have you sold to people like this before? How should you go about connecting with them?

Do you remember the TV commercial featuring scrubbed-bright Missy arriving at college to meet her alternative style roommate? Missy had only pastel clothes to hang in the closet. Her roommate had all black. They agreed they liked a certain computer brand. For us, we hope when they're ready, they'll like our homes, because we like anybody in any flavor who might have the capacity to buy.

Anyway, when prospects are looking at the horizontal site plan display, your salespersons can be looking at them without fear of getting caught. It isn't polite to take a visual inventory of hairstyle, make-up, jewelry, blouse, belt, etc., but it is useful.

Testing their comfort level

There is another wonderful function the horizontal site plan display can perform for you. Let's suppose that as a natural thing to happen, your salesperson starts the conversation standing on the opposite side of the table from the prospects. As the conversation progresses, your salesperson can casually stroll around one corner of the table, so that now the three people are only 90 degrees apart. The question is, What will the prospects do in reaction to the salesperson's move? If they spontaneously move around their corner to keep away from the salesperson, they are sending a definite personal comfort message. Remember the cylinder of personal space from chapter nine? That's what this is all about.

Garage Door Insert

The next investment to make in your budding garage sales center is to remove the roll-up door that's there and replace it with a double French door insert panel. This should be portable so you can use it again, and it needs to have two separate double French doors with maximum glass in each.

To begin with, this door panel is a dead giveaway to prospects driving around that the sales center is located here. It also says to them that they should meet your salesperson inside the garage, rather than going to the front door of the model. Dress this up with signage and an awning in your logo colors, and you'll be in the big time, for sure.

Sales Trap

Some builders like to use a sales trap to encourage their prospects who view the model by themselves to stop back by the sales center before leaving. They do this by installing fencing of some type, projecting out from the garage door insert panel midway between the two sets of French doors. The fencing, then turns at right angles and runs along the front of the model home just outboard of the walkway that we hope passes through the magic spot, remember?

Prospects are then enticed to enter the sales center through the doorway that's outside of the fence line. When they leave the sales center to view the model, they are directed to use the other door, which is inside the fencing. The only way they can then avoid passing back through the sales center is to climb over the fencing. Much the same effect can sometimes be achieved with artfully placed landscaping.

**High touch,
or high tech?**

You may already know how I feel about this idea. To begin with, I would much prefer that your salesperson accompany prospects on the model tour. I realize this may not always be possible, but it is ideal. Second, I am not comfortable with hemming prospects in, which is a lot like pushing them around. It's definitely high tech, not high touch.

Salesperson's Office

Almost every new home salesperson I've ever met feels strongly that one corner of a typical two-car garage sales center should be partitioned off to create a private area for their desk, etc. Their rationale is that they need a private space in which to discuss sensitive personal and financial information with their prospects.

I wonder if it isn't really about making them feel more important because they have a private office at work. My view is that the kitchen of the model home is right around the corner, and families traditionally discuss important family business while sitting at the kitchen table. There is also the living room, with its comfortable seating and coffee table available for this use. Why would you want to cram three people into an office space that at best is 80 square feet in size? One answer would be to make it larger than 80 square feet, but that really begins to eat into the available floor space in the main display area.

While I resist this idea of creating office space in a two-car garage, I have learned to bow gracefully to the inevitable. It's a different matter entirely in a three-car garage. There you have space in abundance. You can even create two private spaces in a three-car garage, one for an office and another for a closing room, if you like.

Laundry Room Doorway

Every garage has a back door into the home, so your garage sales center will have a back door to the model home interior. Most likely, it is a doorway that connects to the laundry area or mud room of your model.

The point here is that this doorway should not be used by salespersons and prospects to enter the model home on their demonstration tour. Doing so destroys all the potential to build the perceived value of the model by approaching it from the front, as we discussed in chapter eight. I recognize that compromises may be appropriate when inclement weather intervenes, but those times should be an exception, not the rule. To encourage good behavior, some builders install a door knob fixture that has no knob on the garage side. Coupled with a gentle spring to close the door by itself, this allows people only to pass through it on the way out of the model, coming back into the sales center to handle the paperwork, so to speak.

Sales Center Displays

Your sales center will have some wall space that you may wish to use to mount displays that will enhance the ability of your sales staff to produce sales. Among these might be the following.

Maps	Map displays can be extremely useful in helping prospects orient themselves to your area and in telling them the story about why your area is a wonderful area in which to live. Be sure to show major roadways, shopping areas, schools, and other aspects that might be particularly interesting to your prospects.
Aerials	Many people find aerial photos to be fascinating, particularly if they reveal interesting features or amenities that are in proximity to your site.
Builder Story	Prospects frequently want to know who you are, what you've done, what you stand for, how you got started, and why they should count on you. Show them.
Homes	It is idiomatic that sales centers include a wall of home elevations paired with their corresponding floor plans. You might think of framing these and mounting them in such a way that they can be taken down for closer examination. Binding your whole collection in several large scrap books is a nifty way to make them portable and focus prospects' attention on one at a time.
Lifestyle	It is always a good idea to show representative members of your target market enjoying life in some home-related activity. Just be sure to be properly representative of diversity. Remember, we love everybody who would like to buy a home from us.
Logo	Believe it or not, prospects forget where they are while they are standing there with you. Remind them with a prominent logo display.
Options	Many builders find that having a rich selection of options and upgrades makes it easier for prospects to choose their homes and easier for the company to make satisfying margins. Let people know that opportunity is available.

If your homes have some distinctive construction-related features that you think significantly set them apart from your competition, you might consider building an example of that element and mounting it as a display in your sales center. I have even seen that done as a substitute for the horizontal site plan display when there was no site plan to display. This might be particularly useful for custom home builders, who pride themselves on craftsmanship and may only build on their customers' homesites. Another example might be our friends in the systems-built business, who have a powerful story to tell about the advantages their approach to home building offers.

Clean and Neat

It seems clear to me that any sales facility you provide should be clean, neat, picked up, and ready for business. Tiffany's, on Fifth Avenue, has a man who polishes their brass name plate outside once an hour, all day long. Take a clue!

The Notebook Sales Center

One of the more notable stories I like to tell in presentations has to do with the notebook alternative to sales center displays. The story opens with me showing a notebook to the audience, opening it up so they can plainly see that there is nothing whatsoever inside. Then, I pick out two or three people in the audience, walk over to them, and open the notebook again so they can see inside from closer up. It is remarkable, to me at least, that I have never encountered anyone who did not look at the notebook, even when they knew there was nothing in there.

This is not to say that they are stupid, for surely they are not. This is to say that people cannot resist looking in a notebook that is opened and held out toward them. I think the imperative to look in that notebook equals the one to answer a ringing phone.

I learned this technique in a timeshare presentation where there was no real estate to show. The sales staff had to come up with a technique they could use to breathe value into that nonexistent real estate, so they came up with the notebook. Early on in their sales presentation, I was asked why I enjoyed coming to this particular location for my vacation each year. I made up the answer that I enjoy saltwater game fishing.

Custom-tailored sales displays

Smoothly, Biff opened his notebook, and there it was: a photo, looking down from a low-flying helicopter, of a Bertram 42 sport fishing boat thundering out to sea! There was green water, white spray, a whole lot of white fiberglass, and a gleaming aluminum tuna tower reaching toward the sky. Down in the cockpit stood the teak fighting chair with the footboards. Seated in the chair, relaxing with a big grin on his face, was their representation of me. I was enthralled.

They showed me my fantasy. The photo even had two boat babes standing on either side leaning over and blowing gently into my ears! Where do I sign?

If I had answered Biff's question by saying I came for the golf, his notebook would have opened up just the same, but to a different picture. This would have been a shot taken at dawn with a camera placed on the grass of a golf course green. In the foreground would have been the cup, a staff projecting upward from it and a hand holding the staff. In the background, I would have seen me having just stroked a putt. It would be clear from the track the ball was leaving in the dew, that it was going to go in. Why? Because that would have been my fantasy.

Show customers their dreams

What do either of these photos have to do with selling real estate? Everything! Are they not fabulous representations of very specific gifts? Especially when there is no real estate to show, romancing the gift is even more important!

There's more. Any displays you put on the walls of a sales center compete with salespersons for the prospect's attention. It really hurts me to think that you would spend lots of money to create displays that are so interesting, your customers would rather look at them than get to know your salesperson.

There again, displays you put on walls have to be appropriate for all prospects who might appear. Notebook displays, on the other hand, can be custom selected for each prospect individually, shown at exactly the right moment and withdrawn when their purpose is fulfilled. This makes notebook sales centers a pretty good idea.

Depicting the Gifts You Offer

Now, take that idea and apply it to the range of gifts you might expect your customers to be looking for. Find a stock photo service and select some beautiful lifestyle photos that illustrate your possible gifts. Then, do the same thing with your prospects that Biff did for me. Turn their attention away from the expensive displays you might not be able to afford anyway, and direct it instead toward the magnetically powerful sales center you hold in your hand.

As a clue to what those gifts might be, I routinely ask Institute of Residential Management students to tell me what the advertising message ought to be when the target audience is first-time home buyers. The set-up goes this way. "We are going to mount a repetitive direct mail advertising campaign targeted at apartment renters. We will be sending multiple pieces, so we can afford to have multiple messages. Tell me, what do we have to offer these folks to entice them to buy one of our homes?" The range of answers include the following:

Privacy   both visual and sound

Investment it will grow in value

Freedom   do what you want with it

Ownership   pride in your own space

Belonging   now, you're a home owner

Security   home owners have rights

Yard space an outside place to enjoy

You get the picture, right? In years of doing this, no one has ever said we should talk about our construction quality or our architectural design. Nobody contributes ad messages that have anything to do with the house itself; it's all about the dreams.

Trailer Sales Centers

You will someday be placed in the position of deciding about setting up a trailer on a new community site to get those presales going before home construction can begin. There are a couple of things you can count on in this situation. The pressure to get started will come from the company principal or the finance types. They're acutely aware of the outlay of cash that was required to secure the land. They can't wait to get the money flowing back in, even if it's just the promise of money flowing back in.

Trailers cannot manufacture demand

Be very careful. More sales trailers have failed than have succeeded. Demand has to be super strong to make them work. If it is that strong, you might better be thinking about holding off sales so you can get higher prices later on. If the worry is that you need to start early to make this deal work, maybe you should be asking whether you should be doing the deal at all.

This is not to say that a sales trailer is always a bad idea, just that you should be very careful. You cannot manufacture demand with a trailer. The demand is either there, or not. If you decide to go ahead, try to make the trailer look not so much like a trailer. Asking customers to step up into an unimproved rental trailer is asking a lot of them. Who knows what could be inside?

I did encounter a situation once that seemed to demand a trailer. It was a failed large lot, custom home subdivision. Everybody in town knew the story about how it failed the first time, and how it had failed again several times hence. Nobody wanted to risk buying if we were just going to fail again.

Erecting an extremely attractive sales center right up front in a dressed-up rented trailer with luxurious landscaping seemed to offer the opportunity to say to all passersby that we were well funded and serious about doing business. It did not take our breaths away with sales production, but it did establish us as genuine businesspersons, serious in intent and worthy of respect, until our spectacular model home could be completed. Many prospects who bought their luxury homes from us several years later first met our team members in that trailer. That part is good, and the decision to use the trailer was correct, but the cost was huge. The point is not to do it unless you have to.

Model Home Interiors

Professionally merchandised models are probably your best marketing investment. Getting quality work done takes quality dollars, for sure, but most builders I have worked with would tell you they recover their investment and more.

**Do it well
or not at all**

That all changes if you try to get the job done on the cheap by a local furniture store or, worst of all, by somebody's wife who is an amateur. A well-finished, well-cleaned empty model home is a much better selling tool than a poorly decorated model could ever be. Unless you are rock sure of your eye for interior design, I would recommend you treat model furnishing like a hand grenade with the pin pulled. Run. Then get expert help.

Even with expert help, be sure to bring salespersons into the loop as design decisions are being made. They can offer extremely valuable customer insights that any professional merchandiser will welcome. Salespersons also need to feel they had a hand in choosing the final design regime. That way they will present it with pride and enthusiasm.

Rely on your merchandiser to review your model home floor plan before you commit it for construction. An experienced merchandiser will be able to offer great advice on plan improvements that result in a better model being built. It's a good deal all around.

Design Centers

It delights me to see design centers take off in popularity. It has long been clear that customers want to dress up their homes and are willing to pay big bucks to do it. More and more builders are stepping away from offering troublesome custom changes in favor of high-profit options and upgrades, clearly another win-win for everybody.

Design center design is becoming a discipline on its own. There is a lot to learn from retailing experts in how to display your offerings for maximum effect. There is also the question of where to locate your design center. More and more multisite builders are opting to locate a bona fide storefront in a high-visibility location and place their corporate design center there in a convenient and high-visibility setting.

I hope we can agree that having tile and carpet samples, and maybe some kitchen cabinet doors leaning against the wall of a secondary bedroom of your model home, is not a design center. This level of presentation doesn't cut it.

Integrated Selling Campus

Not long ago, I came across an integrated selling campus that I think is very impressive. It includes two model homes on adjacent homesites, and a third cleared home site next door offers paved parking space. Let's be clear: This is a facility that supports an on-your-lot building program, so it is intended to last for awhile.

The model homes both feature garages that project out toward the street, and both garages had been extended about ten feet farther forward than normal. The left-hand house has a left-positioned garage, and the right hand house has a right-positioned garage, so that overall, the two homes together present a big "U" shape. The yard space within the "U" has been extensively landscaped in a way that connects both houses, and there is a walkway meandering from one to the other.

An integrated sales and design facility

By extending the left-hand garage 10 feet forward, enough space was gained to create two genuinely private offices in a two-car-wide garage format and still have ample sales floor space left. The right-hand garage next door, being similarly extended, had enough room to put in a really nice design center. What knocked me out was the layout of the design center.

It features a double-kitchen motif, dominated by two kitchen islands. One island has a standard countertop and is placed next to standard cabinets, standard appliances, and standard lighting fixtures. The other island presentation is top-of-the-line.

When customers walk in to work with a staff designer, and no one else is already there, guess which island they sit at. You got it: the upgrade one. If another group arrives, they are forced to sit at the standard one, and they feel deprived. While the new arrivals are feeling low, the first folks are enjoying their superiority, which now they must defend by actually selecting upgrade stuff. Don't you love it?

CHAPTER TWELVE

Getting Everybody on the
SAME PAGE

It is time to think about the role of sales management in getting the sales staff up to speed and integrating their efforts with those of other people in the company. It's time to get everybody on the same page.

Positivism

Throughout this book, I have purposely tested your capability to embrace positivism and consider alternative, high touch ways of doing things. The more cynical of you have probably already put this book down. Good.

Cynicism isn't cool— it's simply poison

There is a strong message here. Cynicism poisons everybody's ability to contribute to the success of the company. As a manager, you cannot engage in it yourself, and you would do well to root it out when you find it in others.

Positivism promotes production, profit, and fun

Most people will rise to the occasion when they sense an opportunity to work in a positive environment where people are interested in their well-being and devoted to helping them fashion a bright and successful future for themselves. Most people would instinctively prefer to work for a company that builds homes the right way and treats its customers with respect and appreciation. From time to time, you will encounter individuals who are not ready to follow this path. Free them to follow another.

Production Versus Sales

In many companies, there seems to be some degree of tension between the folks who build the houses, and those who sell them. Believe it or not, I have heard production people say things like, "Why can't they just sell what we build? Would that be so hard? Just last week, she sold a home with a pink bathroom set in it. She has no idea how hard it will be to find the white set scheduled for that house, get it stopped, send it back, find a pink set, and get it here on time. Likely as not, those knuckleheads will wind up putting it in the wrong house, and I'll have to go through the whole thing all over again. Why can't they just sell what we build"?

Reconcile sales needs with production needs

I've heard salespersons say, "You know, we're really proud of the way our homes are built. We'd like to take our prospects out on the site, but we've learned not to do that. When we drive up and get out of the car, there's at least two radios turned up full blast, one with heavy metal and the other with salsa. There are half-naked, ill-groomed men running around yelling and cursing. Then there's the beer cans and food wrappers lying around, not to mention that funny sweet-smelling blue smoke drifting down toward the creek bottom. We just can't expose our customers to that."

Have you ever heard stuff like that? Folks, I'm here to tell you companies that can't get it together better than this don't last in this business. Here's an alternative story.

Production With Sales

"Let me tell you what happened last week. I had these buyers from Cleveland, see, and they were interested in an Astoria model. We had one under construction, so I called Joe Fuller, the super, and told him I wanted to show the house. Joe met us there, and you know what? He came up and said hello to me by name and asked to be introduced to my customers. He told them we were building this home for the Johnsons, but we'd love to build another one just for them. He gave us all hard hats and advised us to be real careful. He even went along with us for a bit and answered some of their questions. And get this: There were no loud radios, no yelling. I was amazed."

"The folks from Cleveland signed that afternoon for an Astoria on Lot 32."

You Can Do It

Would you rather have the second scenario in your company? You can, you know. It's just a matter of getting salespersons and production folks to realize they're really a team. Get busy.

It's Mostly Leadership

Solving stuff like this—as a matter of fact, running the whole company or any significant operation within the company—is mostly about leadership. Sure, there's always some technical knowledge involved, but home building is not rocket science. You can find people who have the technical knowledge, and you can teach people the technical knowledge they need. This book is an example of that, I hope.

Leadership is hard to find and harder to develop. Without it, no company does well for itself or its customers for very long. Without leadership, you are ultimately doomed.

Sorry, the finger pushing these keys is pointing at you. If not you, then who? It's time to step up.

Authority and Responsibility

This is sometimes a tough idea for some folks to grasp, but it is very important in the proper exercise of leadership. As a manager, you may delegate authority to somebody to perform an action on your behalf, but you cannot escape responsibility for how that action is performed. It is unacceptable to say, "I told him to do it. If it isn't done, go yell at him."

Delegate authority but not responsibility

In the U.S., we are currently plagued by an epidemic of attempted responsibility avoidance. It seems nobody is big enough to step up and say, "I screwed up. I'm sorry." It just makes it more difficult to work together productively if you have folks like this in your midst. Fix it.

A Sense of Team

I am a great fan of using uniform company dress to build a sense of esprit de corps among your team members. One great client of mine has done a particularly fine job of this. Let me describe their program. Perhaps you'll want to emulate it.

To begin with, this company has a distinctive set of strong corporate colors. They "own" their colors among home builders in their region. Their colors are prominent in all newspaper advertising, all billboards, all sales centers, all brochures, all business cards, etc. They publish a great newsletter that—you guessed it—features their corporate colors. Their corporate office reception area and lavish design center feature their corporate colors.

**Company dress
wins every time**

All sales staff members, all office personnel, and all jobsite superintendents have been issued a selection of clothing items in the corporate colors. Because more than one color is involved, not everybody has to wear the same color shirt everyday, but the shirts they wear all have the company's logo embroidered above the pocket. Over time, the company's parking lot has been changing toward the company's colors as individuals purchase new cars or trucks. Around Christmas, senior managers give neat things like corporate color fleece jackets to all employees in thanks for their support.

It's all very good. You better believe our customers pick up on it and remark about it. They see the pride our folks have in the company they represent. Customers understand that these people will deliver a superior product, because they know no other way to work. It's a great investment that pays off big time.

Maslow's Hierarchy of Needs

You can help yourself a lot in getting your associates to act as a coordinated team if you can understand better what is likely to be their big emotional need at the moment. The great granddaddy of insight into employee motivation was Abraham Maslow, who published a book about his famous hierarchy of human needs in the 1950s.[1]

Self-Preservation

The most basic level of human need is the imperative to survive. At this level, food, water, and shelter are of real concern because their supply is not assured. Daily effort is directed to satisfying these most basic needs. There may be little time for anything else.

Sadly, homeless people spend considerable time at this level of existence.

Safety and Security

Once the immediate need for basic survival is reasonable met, concern shifts to preserving its continued supply into the future. The individual now has something to protect and senses the need to plan ahead. The fear of loss is strong, because of the serious injury that would surely follow.

Middle class Americans may find themselves at this level if employment and income are abruptly interrupted. Salespersons on straight commission come to know this level well.

Self-Identification and Socialization

Once individuals feel reasonably safe and secure, their attention broadens to include relating to other people around them. They start wanting to feel they belong to a worthwhile group. Belonging validates their sense of personal worth as being part of something larger than themselves. See why I like uniform company dress?

Self-Esteem

Once belonging is established, people begin to look for recognition of their accomplishments from others in the group. This drives individuals to do things that will be noticed within the group. Fortunately, most people look for something good to do, but bad behavior is often similarly motivated.

---

[1] Maslow, Abraham H. *Motivation and Personality.* New York, Harper and Row, 1954.

The drive to win your sales contest or be recognized as the top producer is an expression of this human need. It's a smart thing to do to reward these accomplishments with trophies as well as adulation and cash.

I have a great client who requires all employees and associates who meet the public to wear name tags. The tags start out black plastic with white engraved lettering. The tags move through a progression of bronze to silver to gold backgrounds as certain defined levels of accomplishment are achieved. It's really neat to see how much motivation and pride those tags create.

Next time you're in a Cracker Barrel restaurant, ask your table server to explain the gold embroidered stars you see on many of the aprons in the dining room.

Self-Fulfillment

The final and highest level of human need is to feel fulfilled inside, to feel like your effort and existence have created some lasting good. People seeking fulfillment are self-motivated by self-satisfaction, and they may curiously care relatively little about what others may think of them. While they may accept and appreciate badges of accomplishment, their real motivating rewards are inside.

The truly effective sales manager will find ways for salespersons to find fulfillment on the job. Otherwise, this highest level of achievement will find expression outside of work, and the company would lose all the value their extra effort could have generated.

What It's Really About

Perhaps you can see now why this book has followed the path it has. I am convinced that salespersons and their managers want to find self-fulfillment in their jobs. Playing the game at the highest level of proficiency and professionalism offers that opportunity, especially if the effort is focused on helping others achieve their dreams. You can help now, by focusing your attention on organizing a true training program in your company, and that's what I will be talking about in the final chapter.

CHAPTER THIRTEEN

Organizing Sales
TRAINING

The original idea of having weekly sales meetings included setting aside some time for conducting ongoing training intended to help salespersons raise their levels of proficiency. In recent years, most sales meetings have been devoted almost exclusively to tracking sales already signed but not yet closed.

Managers review long lists of sales in progress, updating themselves on where buyers are in the mortgage application process, whose color sheets are still outstanding, and why those folks in Vermont haven't sent back their signed change order form yet. By the time that's all done, there is no time or energy left to do any training. Besides, "We are writing as many as we can deliver, anyway. Training can wait."

It's Fulfillment Again

What I described above wasn't a sales meeting. It was a fulfillment meeting. It really bugs me that salespersons and sales managers consume their time dealing with fulfillment issues. I would much rather see the company have a fulfillment coordinator working in liaison with salespersons and sales managers to ride herd on these troublesome details, so that the professional sales experts could work on making more sales. Call that person what you will: closing coordinator, customer service representative, whatever. It's the job I'm concerned about: getting it done well so your buyers are happy and getting it off the backs of salespersons so they can concentrate on selling.

Getting Back to Training

It would please me immensely if you would consider getting back to sales training as a major part of your weekly meeting schedule. There should be enough issues and ideas in this book to give you lots of things to talk about. But, there's even more to include in a well-organized sales training program.

Visiting Trainer

Absolutely consider having an established trainer come work with your staff. I do that sort of work, and I've mentioned others who do also. Look around. There is no shortage of trainers, any of whom would love to work with your staff. All you have to do is pick someone whose style and basic approach to new home sales resonates with your own.

Attending Seminars

Another great thing to do is taking your group to a sales, motivational, or positive-thinking seminar or rally when one is conducted near you. It is a great bonding and morale-building experience for your team. They will thank you for providing the opportunity, I'm sure.

Builders' Shows

Of course, you should consider taking your group to major builders shows for the valuable seminar experiences they include. The National Association of Home Builders' International Builders' Show is the largest one. But remember also the Southeast Building Conference, the Pacific Coast Builders' Conference, and the Atlantic Builders Convention. I have appeared numerous times at all three, and I can testify to their value.

Books and Tapes

There are many books and/or tapes out there that are wonderful resources for your use. Thanks again for buying this one. Please make good use of it.

Getting Maximum Value

When I do sales training, I generally plan on spending three days with your group. Sometimes I do that all at once. Sometimes clients prefer to spread it out over time, so folks don't get blown away. Either way is fine with me.

**Tastes good,
doesn't last**

I have learned, though, that what I often wind up doing is serving wonderful Chinese food. Everybody loves it at the time, but it has no lasting effect. Folks go to work the next day saying, "That was really great!" But, there is no difference in their behavior in selling. This is not satisfactory.

**Getting serious
about training**

So, I generally bring along a copy of my *52-Week Continuing Sales Education Plan* for my clients to use. It goes over every facet of the training I provide, taking students through the process of really learning how to do each step and how to integrate all of the material into their daily work. It's designed to be a detailed agenda for sales training meetings that you conduct yourself for your team members. It includes homework assignments, and it asks your team members to role-play. Too many managers look it over and exclaim they don't have anywhere near enough time to get involved in that level of training. Their competitors rejoice.

Guest Lectures

Because you have not experienced that training, I cannot give you the whole 52-week program to use. I have included, however, one especially valuable component drawn directly from my continuing sales education program. It is a series of guest lectures that you can use to spice up your weekly sales meetings. There is a setup for each one in the pages that follow, so it will be easy for you to recruit and prepare your guest lecturers to share their expertise with your group. It is a very good thing.

A sales presentation portfolio
documents your chosen practices

You'll see references in the coming material about sales presentation portfolios. To my way of thinking, the final job in any sales training program is to review what your trainer advises, step-by-step, and then decide exactly how each step will be done in your company. Then a salesperson is assigned on a rotating basis to write a one-pager on your chosen way and insert it in each salesperson's sales presentation portfolio. When a new person joins your team, just make another copy and give them a month or so to get up to speed. Administer a test or, better yet, a series of tests to measure their progress.

You'll find this valuable resource set in the next chapter. Get going, okay?

CHAPTER FOURTEEN

Presenting Guest
LECTURES

Until you are ready to begin a full-scale weekly training regimen for your team, at least start this guest lecturer series. Visits from these experts will broaden your team's knowledge base and give them rich new insights to add to their sales presentations. The result for you all should be an increase in sales.

Company President (Owner) on Origins, Growth, Current Status, Goals, and Team Building

It is fitting that the first of many guest lecturers that I suggest you invite should be your company president, chief executive officer, or owner, as appropriate. Your company and your staff, including you, have made a substantial commitment to conducting this continuing sales education program, and it will improve the financial performance of the entire company. Your guest today should make that point and underscore the importance of your team members to the success of the entire organization.

It will be a very positive experience for your team members to hear your guest reaffirm that sales, rather than production, drives the company. True, it may seem as though production commands the attention of most of your company management personnel. But, in fact, your staff warrants everyone's respect, because sales make everybody else's job necessary.

Throughout this continuing sales education program, I stress the importance of team building. Today's guest can make a large contribution in this area also. Recalling the early days of the organization and the struggles that early team members undertook to build the organization should make your team members proud to be part of the company.

Everyone is interested in the current status of the company and even more interested in what plans may exist for its future growth. Today's guest should fire up your troops with exciting plans for the future.

Of course, don't miss the opportunity to show off your staff to your guest. The effort that you have devoted thus far to the continuing sales education program should have produced impressive gains in the professional capability of your team members. Your pride in them today will not go unnoticed.

Company Construction Head to Introduce the Upcoming Sessions on Dwelling Structural Components and Systems

Up to now, I have made only slight reference to the necessity of sales professionals to understand how your dwellings are constructed. Now, you should commence a training sequence based on expert guest speakers that should give them a very thorough understanding of dwelling construction, particularly as it relates to the appreciation of the quality and care with which your new homes are built.

Today's guest lecturer should introduce this training module, stressing the importance it holds for successful selling and expressing appreciation for your staff's interest.

If there is not total harmony between the sales department and the construction department of your company, look upon this as an opportunity to build better working relationships. Frequently, construction team members feel that salespersons allow customers to request too many custom features or bother construction team members with too many site visits during working hours. On the other hand, salespersons may feel that construction workers are rude and abusive to prospective purchasers and that the construction department is too stringent regarding special efforts to accommodate prospect's needs.

If this is true in your organization, let each side voice their opinions and complaints, then guide the discussion toward a reasonable compromise.

Mortgage Lender Number One on Loan Programs and Qualifying Procedures

Have your guest this week explain what mortgage products they have to offer you and their current rates. Gather information on current loan programs for inclusion in your sales presentation portfolios.

Make a connection here and now that will keep you up-to-date on these mortgage products in the future. Ask your guest to go into detail on their mortgage-qualifying requirements and procedures. Find out what your guest's company can do with marginally qualified cases. See whether your guest would be willing to share information about any excess qualifying room individual prospects might have. This information, presented to prospects in the form of a "credit card" preloaded with their excess qualifying capacity along with one of your option and upgrade catalogs, can do wonders for your profit ratios.

Closing Coordinator on the Closing Process

Whether you have an internal closing coordinator or utilize the closing services of a mortgage lender, law firm, or title company, invite the person who most directly manages your closing process to meet with your group. The object here is to review the closing process thoroughly, making sure that every one of your team members understands the process completely. Now is the time to deal with any nagging questions that have gone unanswered for any member of your team. Now is also the time to build understanding and respect between your staff and an individual who occupies a strategic position in their quest for sales success.

Go over all of the paperwork and encourage your guest to explain the reasons behind all of the policies and procedures that may seem to be so restrictive. Make sure you discuss any instances where your staff may feel the closing process let them down or where the closing coordinator may feel that members of your team failed to provide professional service.

Construction Superintendent on Reading Blueprints

One of the best methods of building credibility that we have encountered is referring to blueprints for factual answers to questions that prospects raise. Using blueprints is also a very effective rapport-building activity, because most prospects find blueprints exciting. An open set of plans seems to attract a prospect's attention in a very powerful way.

This phenomenon is so predictable and so productive that we teach an entire closing routine around the concept of "returning to the sales office to find the answer you want in the plans." We go so far as to suggest that individual members of your sales staff may be comfortable with the idea of spreading blueprints on the sales office floor, knowing that doing so will eventually draw prospects down to a seated position on the floor alongside the sales representative. At that point, there is very little of the adversarial relationship remaining between prospect and salesperson, because neither can "threaten" the other while seated on the office floor.

Of course, the entire idea of using blueprints to further the sales process will only work if blueprints of your design plans are available in your sales facility and your salespersons are skilled in their use. Therefore, the object of this week's meeting activity is to have your construction superintendent show your salespersons how to read blueprints. Using a full set of construction drawings, your guest lecturer should show your team members how the multiple drawings are organized into subject groups and how to find the page that is most likely to contain the details to answer a particular question. A thorough review of symbology is also a good idea.

You might suggest that your lecturer utilize hypothetical questions to test your representative's ability to find and decipher the applicable drawing.

Outside Closing Agent on the Closing Process from the Lender's Point of View

Previously, you presented the closing process from your company's point of view. Now, it's time to look at the same process from the mortgage lender's point of view. Depending on your individual circumstances, you might want to use a closing agent from a mortgage lender, an attorney's office, or a title company. No matter which is appropriate, the object of this meeting activity is to make sure that your salespersons understand the reasons for all of the procedures and paperwork that will be involved in every mortgage transaction supporting the sales they make. Because every salesperson will acknowledge the importance of the supporting role they wish mortgage loan representatives to adopt, it is equally important that salespersons understand and support the procedures the loan representative must follow. That way, the customer will perceive that the two sides of the transaction are cooperating with one another in a professional manner, and draw the conclusion that the process that they are undergoing as purchasers is normal and comfortable.

Mortgage Lender Number Two on Loan Programs and Secondary Market Operations

As you have done previously, have this week's guest lecturer explain the mortgage programs available from their organization so that your salespersons will continue to broaden their knowledge of current market conditions. Make sure that information on their current loan programs is gathered for inclusion in your sales presentation portfolios.

Ask this week's mortgage representative to explain the process whereby individual new home and resale mortgages are bundled into packages that are sold on the secondary market. This process should help explain why standardization in mortgage underwriting practices is mandatory.

In the past, mortgage lenders anticipated that most loans they originated would be retained in their own portfolios. Now the overwhelming practice in the mortgage business is to package loans for resale. Your salespersons should understand how this process functions and how mortgage loan originators maneuver to protect themselves from fluctuations in market interest rates by hedging positions in the secondary market. Of course, the primary object of secondary market operations is to generate cash from the sale of loans so that new loans can be made in the local market area.

Appliance Supplier or Salesperson on Romancing Appliances

Many team members feel that up to 40% of the perceived value of a new home is contained within the kitchen. Much of that value is present in the appliances that are selected. An excellent way to gain maximum credit for that value in the eyes of your prospects is to demonstrate each major appliance in the model thoroughly and competently.

For help in this regard, turn to a professional appliance salesperson, whose livelihood depends on selling appliances to retail consumers. Perhaps your appliance supplier can perform this demonstration for you, or you may wish to find a "crackerjack" floor salesperson at a local appliance store who would be willing to teach your staff the "tricks of the trade" that are used in the retail appliance sales business.

Your guest lecturer should teach your sales team members how to demonstrate each piece of equipment for maximum impact and value perception. Make sure that a thorough explanation of warranties that are supplied by the appliance manufacturers is included.

Designate a team member to prepare a summary of this guest's presentation for insertion in your sales presentation portfolios next time.

Company Customer Service Coordinator on Inspections, Standards, and Paperwork for Warranties and Customer Satisfaction

Increasingly, new home sales prospects are becoming concerned with the specifics of warranty protection attached to the homes they are considering. An excellent warranty plan can be a major source of perceived value, helping you to make the sale.

Have today's guest lecturer explain thoroughly the specifics of the warranty program offered to your purchasers. Make sure that your sales team members can explain your warranty program quickly, easily, and completely.

Now, have your guest lecturer explain the procedures used in your company to make sure that each new home you deliver meets the standards of construction you have set for yourselves. Your sales staff members will be able to extract maximum perceived value from the warranty program you offer if they are able to explain the series of inspections and quality checks that are applied to each new home your company builds.

Discussion should continue into the procedures that each new home owner will be asked to follow when registering discrepancies or complaints. What should the new home owner expect in terms of service response time? Are requests for service to be directed to the involved salesperson or to a representative of the construction department? How are grievances to be resolved?

This entire discussion should provide material to your sales team that they can use to underscore the credibility of your company. Make sure that someone in your organization is designated to monitor customer satisfaction regarding service requests and complaint resolutions, and that good examples of your performance are made available for use as testimonials in the sales process.

Lender Number Three on Loan Programs and the Savings Bank Business

Of course, today's lender lecturer should talk about phone programs available from their organization. Make sure that your team members add this information to their sales presentation portfolios.

A major objective of this session should be for your sales team members to understand the basic nature and present challenges of what remains of the savings bank business nationwide. Choose an individual who will be able to discuss this subject thoroughly with your team members.

Foundation, Basement, or Concrete Trade Contractor

With the visit of your construction head and the session on demonstrating appliances as preludes, you can now commence your systematic review of the components of residential construction. The idea is to familiarize your sales staff with the material, practices, standards, and personnel involved in the construction of the new homes you sell. With a thorough knowledge, hopefully your sales team members will be able to communicate a sense of value, quality, and reliability to your purchase prospects.

The best team members to infuse a sense of appreciation in the various components of construction are the team members whose livelihood depends on "doing it right." Whatever the individual guest lecturers in this series may lack in "star quality" will be more than made up by the sense of pride they feel in their craftsmanship. It is exactly that quality, as represented in the sparkle in their eyes, that we want your salespersons to capture. They are the ones who will have to convince your prospects that the individual components of construction in your homes and the practices used in building them are substantial and reliable.

This week's guest lecturer should explain your foundation, basement, and masonry systems in complete detail. If possible, arrange a visit to one of your homes under construction where these components are readily visible. Encourage your guest lecturer to brag on the quality of masonry work found in your homes. That bragging will give your staff images, words, and phrases that they will be able to use with their prospects.

Designate a team member to prepare a summary of this guest's presentation for insertion in your sales presentation portfolios at the next meeting.

Attorney on the Principles of Property Transfer and Mortgage Loan Closings

The purpose of this activity is to familiarize your staff with the legal foundation for the procedures followed in closing new home sales and mortgage loan transactions. Understanding the reasons for, and the development of, the procedures they are asked to follow should serve to lessen the aggravation salespersons sometimes feel about these activities.

Besides, an appreciation of the legal underpinnings of property and mortgage loan transactions broadens the professional knowledge base of your salespersons and will allow them to see how the attorney works to protect the interests of the various parties involved. Realizing that many salespersons feel that attorneys exist to make life more difficult, your company's attorney will probably welcome the chance to conduct this lecture for you as a device in smoothing the business relationship between you all.

Lender Number Four on Loan Programs and Commercial Banking

As before, invite this guest to explain thoroughly the residential mortgage loan programs available from their institution. Then invite them to continue on into an explanation of the economics of commercial banking. Developing an appreciation of the differences between commercial banks and other types of lenders will help your sales staff understand the different approaches to mortgage lending sometimes found in these institutions.

Here is another chance to deal with the question of standardization in mortgage loan underwriting fostered by the necessity of being active in mortgage secondary markets. Ask your guest to speak particularly about the problems involved for commercial banks in making long-term mortgage loans and how secondary market operations tend to reduce the risks they face.

Mechanical Contractor on Mechanical Components and Systems

This activity is designed to acquaint your staff with the plumbing systems found in your homes and the nonelectrical components of heating and cooling systems, if applicable. Your guest should explain the rudiments of quality plumbing design, especially as those principles are actually applied in your new homes. Once again, it might be an excellent idea to conduct this activity in one of your homes under construction where plumbing systems might be readily visible.

The discussion should continue on into the design, function, and selection of various plumbing fixtures found in your new homes. If you allow your buyers to choose, this might be an excellent time to discuss the relative merits of the various alternatives you offer for tubs, toilets, sinks, and other fixtures.

Make sure that the discussion continues on to cover the methods used in your community for handling sewage. If septic tank systems are utilized, it is necessary for your sales team members to understand basic design criteria, such as location of septic tanks and drainage fields.

If domestic water supply is an issue in your homes, make sure that this subject is covered also. This is also the time to tour any community-based sewage treatment or water supply facility that may be a part of the product your salespersons are trying to sell.

If oil or gas heating and cooling systems are used in your new homes, now is the time to cover them also. Depending on your situation, another lecturer may be necessary to accomplish this. Keep in mind that electrical systems will be discussed in two weeks' time.

Designate a team member to prepare a summary of this guest's presentation for insertion in your sales presentation portfolios.

Title Insurance Representative

Have this guest explain the origins of, reasons for, and benefits of title insurance. Make sure that the distinction is made between title insurance protection for mortgages and that for individual home owners. Have your guest explain how title insurance companies operate, paying particular attention to the acquisition and maintenance of property-transfer records.

This might be an excellent time for you and your team members to establish a relationship with a title insurer that would grant you access to extremely valuable market research information. Knowing trends in new and resale home sales in your market area is extremely valuable. Also, being able to track transactions in communities that are directly competitive with yours is very helpful.

If, in your situation, title insurance companies are not used, then you might have an attorney visit with you for this session to explain how title searches are conducted so that law firms can issue an "opinion of title," which serves much the same purpose. In particular, have your title insurance representative or attorney speak to the closing services available from their organization, if you use them. Make sure your team members understand the position occupied by such closing agents in the multiple transactions involved between property seller, property purchaser, mortgage lender, and mortgage borrower in the typical new home closing.

Mortgage Broker on Loan Programs and the Mortgage Brokerage Business

The mortgage broker typically performs a function very similar to the independent insurance agent who represents multiple life, accident, or automobile insurers. Have your guest today explain which mortgage investors are represented and what programs they offer at the moment. Typically, the mortgage broker is the purest form of loan underwriter driven by federal requirements for secondary mortgage market participation. Have them explain how they package loans for delivery to their client investors.

Make sure that your guest explains the difference between mortgage brokerage operations and mortgage banks. Typically, mortgage banks close loans with their own funds and seek to retain mortgage servicing after the loans are packaged and sold. Mortgage brokers, on the other hand, neither use their own funds nor seek to retain servicing.

Under what conditions might a creative mortgage broker be very useful to you? What function do they perform in the mortgage market that your sales team members should understand as part of their professional knowledge?

Framing Contractor

Have this guest lecturer explain how the structural loads of your new homes are supported by exterior and interior load-bearing walls. Standing in a typical home that has just been framed, ask your guest to point out signs of quality and attention to detail that build real value for your prospective purchaser.

This is an excellent time to talk about prefabricated trusses or pre-manufactured wall sections if these items are used in your homes. Ask your guest to explain simple techniques that your prospects might use to detect framing shortcomings in other new homes they inspect. For instance, bulging walls, cracks around doorframes or window frames, sagging rooflines, and nonlevel floors are readily detectable if prospects know what to look for. Explaining these techniques can help your salespersons underscore the high quality of framing found in your dwellings.

Designate a team member to prepare a summary of this guest's presentation for insertion in your sales presentation portfolios at the next meeting.

Hazard Insurance Provider

This lecturer should provide your sales team members with the latest rates applicable for various types of home owners' insurance in your area. Beyond that, an explanation of underwriting standards can give valuable insight into safety aspects of new home design and quality of construction. Over the years, construction practices have been developed at the instigation of hazard insurance underwriters to accommodate environmental factors in your part of the country. Knowing how this has transpired in your area will help build an appreciation of the interrelated nature of the home building industry.

Your lecturer should go on to explain different forms of insurance coverage that are available that may be appropriate to individual home purchasers. Your sales team members should be able to speak with some knowledge about insurance-related matters as a service to your prospects. Perhaps your guest today will be able to supply some simple brochures that could be quite helpful in the sales process.

Tax Assessor or Property Appraiser on Property Valuation, Tax Rates, and Government's Employment of Funds

The purpose of this activity is to demonstrate for your staff how real estate taxes are assessed, how property values are fixed, and how tax rates are determined. The object of this is twofold. First, any professional in residential real estate should be knowledgeable about the process of real estate taxation. Second, your sales team members should have sufficient information at hand to estimate with high accuracy the tax assessment and tax payment that your new home purchasers should anticipate.

An introduction to this process, delivered by the public official responsible in your area, is a very useful exercise in building relationships. Not only will your team members have a chance to meet and work with the responsible government official, but the official will have the opportunity to be with interested professional members of the political constituency.

Electrical Systems Contractor

Ask today's guest lecturer to trace the path of major electrical circuits throughout one of your typical home models. Here again, standing in a framed home where electrical devices and wiring have just been installed, can be quite helpful.

Make sure that each member of your team understands the rated capacity of each of your new home models and can explain the operation of your new home models and their electrical distribution panels. If you are using ground fault interrupter circuits in kitchens, baths, and/or other areas of your homes, make sure that the advantages they offer to home owners are clear to your team members. Have your guest lecturer explain other safety devices that are built into your homes' electrical systems.

Lead the discussion onward to cover the electrical portion of heating and cooling systems found in your homes. A discussion of the relationships between heating and cooling capacity on one hand and home size, insulation rating, and other design characteristics on the other can be very useful. You will want your sales team members to be able to build perceived value through an explanation of your electrical system and components, so make sure they get the information they need from this discussion. Be sure to include a discussion of any special category of wiring you may offer, to facilitate Internet access, for instance.

Designate a team member to prepare a summary of this guest's presentation for insertion in your sales presentation portfolios.

Model Merchandiser on Design Philosophy and the Particulars of Your Models

Here is your chance to discuss the details of your model home interiors with the person or persons responsible for creating them. This discussion should commence with an explanation of how your model merchandiser chose a theme and designated individual design elements with an eye to creating a seductively attractive home for your target market. If there is no relationship between your décor and your target market, now is the time to begin correcting this deficiency.

The model merchandiser might do well to make the same "color board"–oriented presentation to your group now that was made some time ago to the person in your company who placed the order. The idea is for your sales staff to understand the design philosophy behind the individual choices your merchandiser made, so that they can better present your model home to your target market prospects.

It would be normal for each member of your staff, to have an opinion about the appropriateness of your model décor or individual elements thereof. To the extent that these opinions represent an appreciation of the likes and dislikes of your target market, they should be communicated clearly to your model merchandiser. In this way, present designs can be modified and future designs drafted to be closer to the desired profile of your target market.

Model merchandisers are often resistant to considering opinions expressed by salespersons that really reflect individual, personal taste. If it is your desire to have input into present and future model designs, now is the chance to begin the process of communication that will make that possible. Your task will be to convince the model merchandiser that input from the sales staff will be tolerable and will actually lead to a better final product.

Building Inspector on Practices, Standards, Requirements, and Signs of Quality

Invite your guest to explain the underlying purpose of building inspections and the specific practices followed in your area. Your team members should come to understand at what points in the construction process inspections are needed. They should also gain an appreciation of what the inspector is looking for with some degree of detail.

Understanding the standards that must be met by the various trade contractors will help your team members relate an appropriate sense of value to their prospect. This can be enhanced by having the inspector relate signs of quality from a third-party point of view, now that you have heard from some of your trade contractors themselves.

Don't overlook the salutary effect of having your building inspector appear as a professional guest of your sales staff. That has probably never happened in your inspector's career. Building a bond with that individual may prove to be very handy sometime in the future when an extraordinary favor may be required to close a sale on time.

Attorney on Deed Restrictions, Neighborhood Associations, and/or Condominium Documents

Each of these three items is designed to protect the happiness of your new home purchasers and to support the value of the property they have purchased. Have your guest explain how these agreements are founded in law, recorded in your area, and enforced in practice.

There is substantial value embedded in agreements of this sort that can be used to great advantage in the selling process. Hopefully, as they apply to your situation, these sorts of documents are well drafted. Often, they are created with little, if any, input from marketing and sales personnel. To the extent that that is true for you, this guest lecture may be the point of beginning of a new relationship that will result in superior examples of these types of agreements in the future.

Make sure that you pass on to your guest any provisions found in your situation that have proven to be troublesome in the sale or operation of your community. This is your chance to interrupt the process whereby documents of this nature are frequently extracted from word processors at law firms with little, if any, regard given to the specifics of the community being planned.

Principal of Your District's Elementary School on Facilities, Programs, and Excellence

As part of their homework in preparation for today's meeting, your sales staff should have visited the elementary school that serves your market area. There is no substitute for their having seen these facilities firsthand and for having had the chance to meet and talk with various members of the school's teaching faculty and administration.

Today's lecturer should be in a position to give a thoughtful discussion of elementary education in terms your staff will find real and useful. Concentrate on the good things. Seek examples of excellence that can be used to create a realistically positive impression of elementary education for your prospects.

Build a bond with your guest so that it will be comfortable for you to refer prospects directly to this individual when they have questions about their children's education. Don't miss the opportunity to impress this individual with the quality of your new homes. After all, some team members moving into an area check out schools before they visit new home sales offices.

Roofing Contractor

In chapter eight, we emphasized the need to build value in the exterior of your new homes, because it is so often overlooked. Roof systems are critical to the home owner's happiness and should be explained to your prospects thoroughly.

Encourage today's lecturer to give you the information your sales team members will need to build perceived value in your roofing systems. Start with the underlying framing system and progress through sheathing, flashing, and final coverage systems in use in your new homes.

Make sure the detail of quality design and construction methods is included in the discussion. If alternative roof coverings are available, everyone should understand the relative advantages and disadvantages of each. You might even want the discussion to continue on into the esthetics involved in color choices.

Designate a team member to prepare a summary of this guest's presentation for insertion in your sales presentation portfolios at the next meting.

Accountant on Tax and Investment Implications of Homeownership

We have discussed previously the matter of ad valorem taxation of real estate. Now, add to the professional knowledge base of your sales team members by conducting a thorough discussion of the income tax implications of homeownership. Ask your accountant guest to cover this issue in detail and move into a discussion of the investment implications of a new home purchase.

This sort of information will be very useful as your sales team counsels their prospects, giving them rational support in making what we all know is fundamentally an emotional decision to purchase. Of course, we need to be careful about making investment forecasts that may mislead the public, but there should be no problem in providing an approved "ownership analysis" form for use as a closing tool. Today's guest can be very useful to you in formulating such a closing tool and counseling you on its appropriate use.

Principal of Your District's Middle School on Facilities, Programs, and Excellence

In your suggested program of school visitations and reciprocal lectures, we are trying to create a situation where each of your team members will be able to explain the high quality of education available to your new home prospects in a manner uniquely suited to their RUESAP profiles (see chapter 8), set an appointment for prospects to visit with key school officials, and be warmly greeted as a respected professional when visiting a school with a prospect family. Today's session should continue that process, which commenced three weeks ago.

As before, encourage today's visitor to discuss points of excellence that are present in the middle school serving your market area. These should include not only activities and facilities, but also individual educators whose performance and talents are extraordinary. I have found it to be much more productive to deal with the overall question of quality of schools in such specific terms, rather than making a general assertion that, "Our schools are wonderful."

Drywall Contractor

Here is an opportunity for your guest lecturer to explain to your sales team members the signs of quality in a drywall installation. They should all understand the multistep process required to create a flat and seamless interior wall surface.

Make sure that you cover interior ceiling systems also, paying particular attention to the finish that you specify. If alternative ceiling finishes are available, discuss the relative advantages and disadvantages of each from the builder's point of view as well as the home owner's. Finally, cover water-resistant drywall products that are used in the wet areas of the home.

Designate a team member to prepare a summary of this guest's presentation for insertion in your sales presentation portfolios.

Principal of Your District's High School on Facilities, Programs, and Excellence

As before, encourage your visitor today to speak about the positive points of excellence in education offered in your local high school. Since the curriculum and extracurricular activities are likely to be broader than for middle or elementary schools, you may wish to allocate extra time to today's discussion. Make sure that sports are addressed, along with enrichment courses and the core college preparatory curriculum.

Cabinetry and Finish Carpentry Contractor

This is the chance to have your guest lecturer continue the process of educating your sales staff on the finer points of construction quality by explaining what to look for in fine cabinetry and finish carpentry. Capture the points of quality evaluation that your guest explains and use them to compile a checklist. Have your guest describe the aspects of poor quality work also, and end by explaining the level of quality you should expect to see in your homes and why that level is appropriate.

Designate a team member to prepare a summary of this guest's presentation, including checklist, for insertion in your sales presentation portfolios at the next meeting.

Exterior Siding or Pool and Spa Contractor/Supplier

Make a choice based on relevance to your situation or have both specialties represented. Either way, the object is to have an individual who is knowledgeable about either specialty explain to your group how a quality job is done, how to judge the level of quality by looking at the finished job, and what benefits should accrue to a home owner because the job on their home was done right. Make sure to capture the high points in notes that can be distributed to your group later.

Designate a team member to prepare a summary of this guest's presentation for insertion in your sales presentation portfolios.

Police Officer or Sheriff's Deputy on Neighborhood Watch and Residence Security Options

You have the opportunity to accomplish several very important objectives with this presentation. You will make a friend in local law enforcement. You will establish the existence of your community and your sales force with this officer. You will get up-to-date information on neighborhood security practices that will be good to include in your sales presentations. You will also have a chance to discuss personal security issues for your sales staff.

Please emphasize the critical nature of personal security for your sales team members. Nothing will put you out of business faster than having one of your salespersons attacked on your site. Use this opportunity to make it clear to all your team members that guarding their personal well-being is the most important responsibility they have.

Building Inspector on Final Inspections and Certificates of Occupancy

This is a follow-up presentation to the one regarding the stages of construction requiring inspection. Now, it's the final inspection and the granting of a certificate of occupancy that is our concern.

Ask your guest to describe the legitimate reasons for requiring final inspections and certificates of occupancy. The message you'll get will deal with public safety, health, and welfare. All are good themes to emphasize in your selling presentations, particularly with amiables, who need lots or reassurance (see chapter 9).

Ask your guest also to explain how final inspections are scheduled and made. What particular things do inspectors look for? What incredible lapses have they observed? What is the paperwork flow that leads to granting a certificate of occupancy? What are the legal ramifications of a certificate of occupancy?

Local Cooperating Realtor on Builder-Realtor Relations

Long ago, we learned that it's better to get Realtors to tell you how to win their support than attempting to devise Realtor-incentive programs on your own. So it is with the general nature of builder-Realtor relations. Ask your guest to be honest and forthright about what they see to be the strengths and challenges to be in the general relationship between builders and Realtors in your market area. If there are any grievances, let them be aired. Then try to get past them to propose remedies.

Don't let this chance to create a special bond with your guest get away from you. Who knows what might result from this discussion? Perhaps you'll do more business together. Perhaps you'll decide to mobilize the local home builder association and the local Realtor organization to develop and adopt a general builder-Realtor accord that will set the standards for co-op business practices in your market.

Local Cooperating Realtor on Joint Promotional Programs

Select a guest for today whom you think will be willing to develop some specifics on how your two companies might be able to work together for your mutual benefit. That does not mean you have to list all your houses with them, just figure out how you might have a special relationship of trust and support. Maybe you could host a joint open house, do some joint print advertising, work together on a charitable program—who knows? The idea is to create a strategic alliance of sorts that would allow you both to benefit.

Of course, the simplest idea is to make sure all associates of the Realtor firm know they will be welcome and treated well when they bring "clients" to see your homes. And if your two firms have worked out their own Realtor-builder accord that makes clear how your transactions will be handled, assure them that the business you do together will be pleasurable as well as profitable.

Advertising Agency Account Executive on Your Advertising Message Content and Media Placement

Many times, sales team members feel that they are disconnected from the process of creating their advertising message and have no say in determining what is run and where it is placed. They live by your advertising effectiveness, though, so here's your chance to connect them to your advertising program. Having your account executive or creative person present their work and ideas to a savvy sales team will be a good reality check from a knowledgeable source. After all, salespersons talk to prospects about your advertising and are in a good position to judge its effectiveness. The idea here, of course, is to put salespersons together with advertising professionals in the hope that something good will happen.

Now that your team members are familiar with consumer psychographics, as represented by the values and lifestyles (VALS) typology from SRI International (see chapter 7), they are in a position to query your advertising person on how their work on your behalf relates to the psychographic preferences of your target market. Don't be entirely surprised if your advertising person is not fully up to speed on VALS. It's interesting how few advertising professionals have actually received significant academic training in their profession. This may be your opportunity to lead your person into a new area that will help you both tremendously.

It would probably be wise to discuss VALS with your invitee before their visit so they will not be embarrassed in front of your team members.

Your Advertising Agency Account Executive on Your Collateral Material

Last week, you discussed your advertising content and media placement with a representative of the folks who create it. This week, it's time to discuss your brochures and other collateral material in a similar way to make sure they convey a message and style that is consistent with your advertising.

Now that your team members are familiar with consumer psychographics, as represented by the VALS typology from SRI International, they are in a position to query your advertising person on how their work on your behalf relates to the psychographic preferences of your target market.

Land Development Engineer on Establishing the Characteristics of Undeveloped Land as the Beginning of Effective Land Planning

This is an excellent opportunity for your team members to increase their knowledge about the engineering foundations of good community land planning. There is only so much any parcel can provide in support for your community's land plan. Understanding the opportunities, limitations, principles, and costs involved will help your group convey the value of your homesites an a more credible and convincing manner.

Land Planner on Making the Best Community Possible on the Land You Have to Work With

If your engineer guest talked more about drainage and land balancing, perhaps this week's will be more artistic in an explanation of current design trends in residential community land planning and how those aspects of land development can increase the appeal of your community to its intended target market. This is where the relationship between your home owners and their community is created. Your design team needs to have feedback from your sales team on how they did. Your sales team needs to have a fuller understanding on what the design team decided to do, so that the sales presentations they make will be stronger on this aspect of your community's value.

Now that your team members are familiar with consumer psychographics, as represented by the VALS typology from SRI International, they are in a position to discuss with your land planner how the features and benefits of your land plan relate to the psychographic preferences of your target market.

An Authority on Federal, State, and Local Requirements for Residential Construction

Energy efficiency is a long-term subject of interest to home owners. They tend to focus on energy efficiency as it relates to operating costs, but there are significant residential design impacts as well. Many prospective home owners are not aware that they may not be able to have their home designed the way they would want it to be because of regulations imposed by various levels of government. Your guest lecturer today should be able to address the whole range of energy-related topics so your sales team will have a better grasp of this important subject. In particular, be sure to cover the specifics of your own energy-related construction specifications.

Your Architect on Residential Design Objectives Related to VALS Housing Preferences

Your architect or home designer has devoted considerable effort to creating a portfolio of design plans and associated elevations to fill what they perceive to be your target market's range of preferences. This work may have been done with consumer psychographics in mind, but most likely it was not. You should be able to have a very interesting discussion today—passing knowledge and understanding back and forth—in a process that may result in design-related proposals that will improve the value of your product line to your intended target market. Let today's discussion be the start of something really significant for your company.

Lender Number One for a Loan Program Update

This should be a brief update on current programs from your number one mortgage source. If this person visited you for their first guest lecture experience, consider taking your group to visit their office this time around. Making sure your relationship is benefiting fully from the insights provided by visiting one another in your respective places of business is a central idea.

Lender Number Two for a Loan Program Update

This should be a brief update on current programs from your number two mortgage source. If this person visited you for their first guest lecture experience, consider taking your group to visit their office this time around. Making sure your relationship is benefiting fully from the insights provided by visiting one another in your respective places of business is a central idea.

Lender Number Three for a Loan Program Update

This should be a brief update on current programs from your number three mortgage source. If this person visited you for their first guest lecture experience, consider taking your group to visit their office this time around. Making sure your relationship is benefiting fully from the insights provided by visiting one another in your respective places of business is a central idea.

Lender Number Four for a Loan Program Update

This should be a brief update on current programs from your number four mortgage source. If this person visited you for their first guest lecture experience, consider taking your group to visit their office this time around. Making sure your relationship is benefiting fully from the insights provided by visiting one another in your respective places of business is a central idea.

Lender Number Five for a Loan Program Update

This should be a brief update on current programs from your number five mortgage source. If this person visited you for their first guest lecture experience, consider taking your group to visit their office this time around. Making sure your relationship is benefiting fully from the insights provided by visiting one another in your respective places of business is a central idea.

Planning and Zoning Official on Public Policy Objectives Versus New Home Costs

This is your chance to have a planning and zoning official explain to you in your place of business the balance between public policy objectives and the costs of implementing those objectives that works to increase new home prices. Ask this person to come with a list of those sorts of public policies in effect in your jurisdiction and an estimate of the cost that each adds to the homes you build. You come prepared with some data on family incomes in your area and the relationship between those incomes and the ability to qualify for mortgages sufficient to finance the purchase of homes in your price range. What you are driving for is some perception of the number of families who are forced out of your market by the cost of governmental regulations, with the idea of deciding whether what's gained is worth what it costs.

County or City Commissioner on Public Policy Versus New Home Costs

Last week's guest participated in a discussion of what's gained and what's lost by the action of public policy initiatives aimed at restricting the development of new home communities. This week, your guest should address the question of how such regulations implement what the people want. Exactly what is it that the people want? Is it really environmental control? If so, what specific benefits are accruing to the public's welfare because of the imposition of these initiatives? This should be a lively discussion.

County Agent on Dwelling Landscaping Choices And Maintenance

After a couple of emotionally charged discussions of public policy, now it's time to explore a subject where local government has something of real benefit to offer you at essentially no cost. Your local county agent will bring a wealth of knowledge about ornamental plants and their behavior in your area. This person may be so good, you'll want to ask them back to speak at a home owner's meeting.

INDEX

A

accountant, 132
advertising, 136–137
  agency, 136–137
  to establish brand, 21, 24, 78, 110
  as source of prospects, 93, 103
appliances, 121–122
appraiser, 120
architect(s), 5, 138
architectural preference, 18, 47–48
attire, 39, 46, 110
attitude, 43–44
attorney, 130
attributes, product, 42

B

baseball, 43
behavior, observable, 74, 76
BMW, 19, 20, 24, 47, 77
body language, 72–73
BOLT. *See* Bulls, Owls, Lambs, and Tigers
branding, 20–22, 27
builder story, 100
building inspector, 130, 135
Building the Sale, 53–69
  close, 64–67
  delivery, 70
  demonstrate, 57–61
  evaluate, 54–57
  follow-Up, 67–69
  outreach, 69
  resolve, 62–64
  select, 62–64
  welcome, 53–54
Bulls, Owls, Lambs, and Tigers (BOLT), 56, 74

C

campus, sales, 106
carpentry contractor, 133–134
Clarke, Charles, MIRM, 56, 76
close, the, 64–67, 82
  Four Step, 65–66
  tricky, 14, 15, 52
closing, 13–14
  agent, 120–121
  coordinator, 119
Collins, Jim, 9, 50
communication, nonverbal, 72–73
computer(s), in prospect management, 68, 93–94
concrete contractor, 123
confidence, in yourself, 11–12, 52, 64, 82, 84
cooling system(s), 128–129
costs, opportunity, 6
county,
  agent, 140
  commissioner, 140
customers,
  appreciation of, 36
  expectations, 18
  focus on, 12–14, 31–33, 39–44, 53
  persuasion of, 51–52
  profile, RUESAP, 54–56, 65

D

data dumping, 57
delivery, 70
design center(s), 105
differentiation, creating positive, 17–20,
DISC profile, 74
display(s), sales center, 96–103
dress, professional, 39, 46
drywall contractor, 133
dynamics, market, 18

E

Eastern thought, 11–13
    vs. Western, 12–13, 14
electrical systems contractor, 128–129
engineer, 137
experience, shopping, 42

F

follow-up, 67–69, 93–94
foundation contractor, 123–124
framing contractor, 127
fulfillment, of sales, 5–6, 35, 113

G

garage sales centers, 59, 95–99, 106
gift, the, 24–27, 46, 50, 56, 65–67, 78,
    102–103
gratification, 14, 77–78

H

high tech, 30–32, 37–38, 92, 94, 98
high touch, 29–38, 40, 42, 53, 65, 92, 94,
    98, 107

I

inspector, building, 130, 135
insurance, 126, 127–128
Internet, 69–70, 90, 129

J

jai-alai, 43, 95

K

"Karate Kid, The", 10

kinesics, 72–73

L

land planner, 137–138
landscaping, 58, 98, 104, 140
leadership, 10, 28, 109
lenders, mortgage, 119, 120–121, 124, 139
logo, 98, 100, 110
loss, fear of, 63, 111

M

magic spot, 58–60, 98
margin, profit, 2, 18–20, 23, 37
Maslow, Abraham, 110–111
masonry, 124
master chief, 40–43
mechanical contractor, 125
media placement, 136
meeting(s), sales, 13, 35, 113, 115
Megatrends, 29–30
merchandisers, 5, 105, 129–130
merchandised models, 104
Milesbrand, 21
Miles, David, 21
mirroring, 83–84
model homes, 104–105
mortgages lenders, 119, 120–121, 124, 139
Myers-Briggs, 74, 76

N

Naisbitt, John, 29–30
negotiation, 80–82
neurolinguistic programming (NLP), 24,
    83–84
notebook, sales presentation, 26, 101–103

O

objection(s), resolving 61–62, 65, 72
office, salesperson's, 98–99, 106
options, 48, 100, 105
outreach, 69
ownership, 19, 103

P

PAC. *See* Prospect Action Control

"Perfect Storm, The", 3
personal space, 59–61
persuasion, 51, 83
photo(s),
    aerial, 100
    lifestyle, 26–27, 102–013
    of model, 34
plan(s) design, 63, 120, 138
police, 134
pool, 26, 134
portfolio, presentation, 116
positioning, product, 76–80
positivism, positive attitude, 43–44, 107
powers, of negotiation, 81–82
product differentiation, 17–22, 39
prospect,
    grading, 89–91
    follow-up, 67–69, 93–94
    management, 85–94
    registration, 92
    reporting, 86–87
Prospect Action Control (PAC), 68, 93–94
proxemics, 72
psychographics, 47–49, 76, 136
psychology, 56, 83
public relations, 21

Q
question, tie down, 62, 66, 72

R
rapport, building, 12, 40, 42, 53, 65, 67,
    82, 84, 119
ratio, sales conversion, 67, 88–89
ready, willing, and able, 69, 89, 91
Realtor, 2, 135–136
Rector, Clark, MIRM, 20
referrals, 35–36
registration, guest, 92
Richey, Tom, MIRM, 55
Ritz-Carlton, 36
Rolex, 19, 24, 47
roofing contractor, 131
RUESAP, 54–56, 57, 65

S
safety, 34, 35, 111, 127, 128
sales centers, 43, 48, 56, 95
    design of, 96, 106
    displays in, 99–101
    garage, 59, 95–99, 106
    hours of, 34
    traffic in, 87, 91–92
    trailers, 103
sales conversion ratios, 67, 88–89
sales notebook, 26, 101–103
school(s), 21, 100, 131, 132, 133
Schultz, Bob, MIRM, 49
security, 35, 103, 111, 134
self-confidence, 11–12, 52, 64, 82, 84
self-esteem, 111
self-fulfillment, 112
self-identification, 111
self-preservation, 111
share, market, 2, 18, 20, 21, 37, 46
showing, the model, 58–61
siding contractor, 134
site plan display, 76, 96–97, 101
Social Style Grid, 56, 74–76
software system, 68, 93
spa contractor, 134
spontaneity, 12, 64
spot, magic, 58–59
SRI International, 46, 56
superintendent, construction, 110, 118,
    119–120

T
tax,
    assessor, 128
    real estate, 132
tech, high, 30–32, 37–38, 92, 94, 98
technique, mastery of, 10–11, 16, 44, 50, 52
title insurance, 126
touch, high, 29–38, 40, 42, 44, 53, 65, 92,
    94, 98, 107
trailers, 103
trainers, sales, 14, 46, 114
trap, sales, 98
truth, importance of, 44, 79, 87–88

U

urgency, sense of, 54–55, 63, 65, 90

V

validation, 19
value, creating, 2
Values and Lifestyles (VALS) Program,
    46, 56, 136–37, 138
visualization, 24, 66, 83
voicemail, 30–32

W

Walgreen's, 19
warranty, 122
wax, on and off, 10, 12
web site, 69
welcome, 33, 53–54, 65
Western thought, vs. Eastern, 12–13, 14

Z

Zen, 11
zoning official, 140